Routledge Revivals

Thomas Heywood's Pageants

Thomas Heywood's Pageants

A Critical Edition

The Renaissance Imagination
Volume 16

Edited by

David M. Bergeron

First published in 1986 by Garland Publishing, Inc.

This edition first published in 2019 by Routledge
2 Park Square, Milton Park, Abingdon, Oxon, OX14 4RN
and by Routledge
52 Vanderbilt Avenue, New York, NY 10017, USA

Routledge is an imprint of the Taylor & Francis Group, an informa business

Publisher's Note
The publisher has gone to great lengths to ensure the quality of this reprint but points out that some imperfections in the original copies may be apparent.

Disclaimer
The publisher has made every effort to trace copyright holders and welcomes correspondence from those they have been unable to contact.
A Library of Congress record exists under ISBN:

ISBN 13: 978-0-367-19158-0 (hbk)
ISBN 13: 978-0-429-20080-9 (ebk)

The Renaissance Imagination
Important Literary and Theatrical Texts
from the Late Middle Ages
through the Seventeenth Century

Stephen Orgel
Editor

Volumes in the Series

THOMAS HEYWOOD'S PAGEANTS

A critical edition

edited by
David M. Bergeron

The Renaissance Imagination
Volume 16

GARLAND PUBLISHING, INC.
NEW YORK & LONDON
1986

Library of Congress Cataloging-in-Publication Data

Heywood, Thomas, d. 1641.
  Thomas Heywood's pageants.

  (The Renaissance imagination ; v. 16)
  Contents: Introduction—Londons jus honorarium—
Londini artium & scientiarum scaturigo—[etc.]
  1. Pageants—England—London. I. Bergeron, David
Moore. II. Title. III. Series.
PR2572.B47 1986   822'.3   86-12156
ISBN 0-8240-5464-4 (alk. paper)

Printed on acid-free, 250-year-life paper
Manufactured in the United States of America

Contents

Contents

Preface

This critical edition constitutes the first time that Thomas Heywood's pageant texts have all been edited and brought together in a single volume. By making such texts available in a reliable edition, I hope that students of Heywood and of English Renaissance drama will be encouraged to study anew these street entertainments and the one fragmentary masque included here. Heywood was an extraordinarily prolific and often rich writer, but his pageants have received relatively little attention. These pageants of the 1630s, however, represent one of his major dramatic activities in the last decade of his long and productive career.

My editorial duties have been made easier by the help of a number of people, whom I cheerfully cite. Again, I get to thank Stephen Orgel for asking me to do this edition. Many years ago at the invitation of the late Arthur Brown, I had actually begun an edition of Heywood's pageants. Arthur kindly shared his information about these texts with me. His confidence in my ability to cope with Heywood has finally come to fruition. My friends Richard Hardin and Geraldo U. de Sousa helped in many ways, especially by reading and commenting on the Introduction. To my colleagues in the Classics Department at the University of Kansas, Oliver Phillips and Michael Shaw, I am indebted for their kind help in struggling with Heywood's considerable Latin and lesser Greek.

As with my earlier edition of Anthony Munday's pageants, I am again profoundly indebted to Sandee Kennedy, whose competence and patience in preparing the typescript were boundless. Judy Verhage and Georgia Rider kindly assisted in some final matters of preparing the manuscript. For all the assistance that I have received, I am sincerely grateful.

I am pleased also to record thanks to several libraries that made copies of Heywood's texts available to me. I spent some time working on Heywood at the Folger Shakespeare Library, Washington, D.C. The final stages of the research were completed at the University of Kansas in the Watson Library and the Special Collections Department of the Spencer Research Library. I am also grateful for support from the General Research Fund of the University of Kansas that enabled me to bring this project to a conclusion. The photographs of the title pages included here come from the collection at the Henry E. Huntington Library, San Marino, California. They have kindly granted permission to reproduce them in this edition.

David M. Bergeron
University of Kansas

Introduction

By the 1630s, the only literary form--or certainly the only dramatic form--that Thomas Heywood had not dabbled in was civic and court pageantry. But during this final complete decade of his life, Heywood made up for lost time by writing seven Lord Mayor's Shows and at least one masque, of which only a fragment remains. This edition reprints the texts of those mayoral pageants and the fragmentary masque. Heywood's own boast in the preface to The English Traveller (1633) was that he had had a hand or at least a finger in the writing of 220 plays. And he was not yet finished. But this does not even take into account his innumerable prose tracts and poems. His career in the theater alone spans a fifty-year period, from the 1590s to 1640--the greatest period of English drama. For better and sometimes for worse, Heywood was a writer, apparently relishing new or different literary forms, and impressive in his productivity and variety, embodying thereby the Renaissance delight in multiplicity.

Lord Mayor's Shows had become an annual celebration at the inauguration of the new mayor of London each 29th of October since the mid-sixteenth century. Prior to Heywood, such dramatists as George Peele, Anthony Munday, Thomas Dekker, Thomas Middleton, and John Webster had written these pageants. Heywood continues the tradition of major dramatists' preparing the mayoral entertainments. Such pageants were processions through the City of London with tableaux vivants; some of the shows also included dramatic entertainment on the Thames. Trying to understand the complete career of these major dramatists involves some assessment of their pageant writing, but too often critics have paid little heed to these "toyes," as Bacon might call them.

Book-length studies of Heywood have, for example, said little about his pageant career. A. M. Clark gives roughly six pages to a discussion of the mayoral shows, noting, for example: "Originality in Lord Mayors' pageants would have been misunderstood in Heywood's day, and he did not try the experiment."[1] This witty statement also carries a note of condescension that is accepted in all theater histories written by the time that Clark makes his observation. Clark refers to Heywood's recondite, pedagogic, turgid, and clumsy style in the pageants (p. 118)--hardly a judgment that invites closer investigation into the pageants--though Clark concedes that Heywood apparently, however, "pleased the authorities as much as did the

efforts of any of his contemporaries." Boas' later study of Heywood
also devotes six pages to the pageants--presumably the requisite
number of pages for this subject.[2] But Boas, despite Clark's earlier
book, apparently did not know of the existence of the 1638 and 1639
Lord Mayor's Shows. Had he known of them, he might have squeezed out
another page or two.

More recently, books on Heywood have given even less attention to
Heywood's pageant career. Though Grivelet has a somewhat sympathetic
perspective on the pageants, he has little to say.[3] By the time that
we reach the latest book, that by Barbara Baines, we're down to a
handful of sentences about Heywood's pageant career. Baines writes:
"The first three of the seven pageants that Heywood wrote from 1631
to 1639 for the installation of the Lord Mayor of London also offered
the playwright a rehearsal of devices for Love's Mistress in that
they were mythological allegories requiring the services of a master
of scenery and special effects, Garrett Christmas."[4] This statement
suggests that a possible value for examining the pageants rests in
their function as a "rehearsal" for Heywood's play Love's Mistress,
which contains many pageant-masque elements. I doubt that Heywood
saw the matter quite this way. I do not mean to be either churlish
or unappreciative of the book-length studies of Heywood, but there is
the obvious danger that the next book will not so much as mention the
pageants.

This present edition will make it easier for students of Heywood
to examine for themselves all the pageant texts--not previously
possible because the 1874 Heywood edition does not include them all.
Then there may be a basis for determining whether the individual
critic finds anything of value in these entertainments. Because I
have elsewhere written on the subject of Heywood's pageants, I do not
want merely to cover the same territory.[5] I would, however, like to
make a case for a measure of originality in Heywood's pageants, which
reveal some emphases not common elsewhere in his drama.

I begin by noting several somewhat unusual practices or events in
Heywood's pageants. These observations appear either in the texts
themselves or in my commentary notes, but I pull them together here
in order to highlight their significance. First, the 1630s
apparently mark the preeminence of the artificer in negotiations with
the guild; that is, Gerard Christmas, with a long involvement in
civic pageants already behind him, became the principal negotiator
with the guilds. Thus, in 1631, Christmas received a total payment
of £200 from the Haberdashers, out of which he presumably paid
Heywood, who faithfully and regularly praises the talent of Christmas
at the end of each text. The sons, John and Mathias, who succeeded
their father after his death in 1634, collaborated in 1635, for
example, with Heywood to underbid Robert Norman and John Taylor and
successfully had their plan for the Lord Mayor's Show accepted by the
Ironmongers.

Recognizing the crucial importance of these artificers and their considerable talent, Heywood at the end of the 1639 pageant praises the Christmas brothers as "the exquisite contrivers of these Triumphall Modells." Heywood adds: "their workeman-ship exceeds what I can expresse in words. . . ." The triumph of the artificer in the 1630s comes in part from the simple fact that the Christmas family had a long and satisfactory career as artificers in these pageants. They embodied a continuity in dealing with the guilds that Heywood, or any other dramatist, could not immediately match. Interpreting the evidence, one concludes that the relationship between Heywood and the Christmas family was apparently amicable, lacking the tension and conflict that, for example, existed in the working relationship of Jonson and Inigo Jones in the court masque.

More than any other pageant dramatist, Heywood in his texts describes his experience with the guilds, thereby offering insight at least into a dramatist's perspective on how writers dealt with their patrons. I cite some typical examples. In the 1631 text Heywood reveals something of the procedure. He writes: "I cannot heare forget that in the presentment of my papers to the Master, Wardens, and Committies of this Right Worshipfull Company of the Haberdashers . . . nothing here devised or expressed was any way forraigne unto them. . . ." Heywood continues by praising the knowledge of the guild members in understanding what he proposed. Heywood concludes that "they neglect not the studdy of arts, and practise of literature in private. . . ." Even allowing for some exaggeration, one gains a picture of a sympathetic and knowledgeable committee of the guild to whom Heywood made a presentation of his pageant project.

Characterizing his relationship to the guild, Heywood in the 1633 pageant text invokes the cause of modesty lest he "might incurre the imputation of flattery" in praise of the Clothworkers, who, interestingly, in 1634 gave John Taylor the task of writing the mayoral pageant. In describing the working arrangement, Heywood commends the committee's "affability and courtesie, especially unto my selfe being at that time to them all a meere stranger, who when I read my (then unperfect) Papers, were as able to judge of them, as attentively to heare them. . . ." Because the guild had its own reputation to think about, as Heywood notes, they were inclined to be generous in expenditure and also to be concerned about the dramatist's concept for the pageant. Apparently Heywood appeared before the committee with an outline, sketch, or early draft--what he calls his "unperfect papers." From such a presentation serious negotiations began.

In the final pageant (1639) Heywood sketches his "poetic," that is, his artistic strategy in deriving a concept for the pageant. Praising the Drapers, Heywood writes: ". . . in all my writing I labour to avoyd what is Abstruse or obsolete: so withall I study not to meddle with what is too frequent and common." In working out a commentary on Heywood's texts, I can readily testify that he did not always succeed in avoiding the "Abstruse or obsolete"--such "failure" often accompanies poets' statements of intention. But as a principle underlying the entertainment for masses of citizens lining the streets of London, Heywood's statement makes perfectly good sense. He consistently reveals more about his experiences and his ideas for the pageants than does any earlier pageant dramatist. In Heywood's texts we catch a glimpse into the workaday world of a dramatist trying to sell his wares, in this case to an understanding patron.

Heywood consciously includes in the texts of several pageants information about a dramatic scene that exists only to amuse the "vulgar," a tableau that has no other reason for existing. Ordinarily, pageant texts do not describe such materials even if we have every reason to imagine that they were a staple of street shows. First in the 1632 pageant and then in three others Heywood calls attention to the special episode. Heywood writes about the third tableau that appeared in the streets: "This is more Mimicall then Materiall, and inserted for the Vulgar, who rather love to feast their eyes, then to banquet their eares." Because Heywood does not describe the episode, we can only wonder about its exact nature.

But in the 1633 pageant <u>Londini Emporia</u>, Heywood uses a term that connects such non-verbal episodes to another dramatic tradition. Heywood observes of this third show on land that "without some such intruded Anti-maske, many who carry their eares in their eyes, will not sticke to say, I will not give a pinne for the Show. Since therefore it consists onely in motion, agitation and action, . . . in vaine should I imploy a speaker, where I presuppose all his words would be drown'd in noyse and laughter. . . ." The key term "anti-maske," the only use of this term in civic pageants, reflects Heywood's understanding of this concept in the court masque and raises teasing questions about the interrelationship of street and court entertainments.

Heywood uses such intruded business again in the 1635 and 1637 pageants. In the latter he opens another line of defense for these episodes. He writes of this show of "Anticke gesticulations, dances, and other Mimicke postures" that he imitates custom (primarily established by him, one notes). Such a practice should not be censured "especially in such a confluence, where all Degrees, Ages, and Sexes are assembled, every of them looking to bee presented with some fancy or other, according to their expectations and humours." In a word, Heywood recognizes the mixed and diverse nature of the audience. To mix serious and comical matter puts Heywood right in line with public theater practice where performances of whimsical jigs often punctuated profound tragedies. Here and in Heywood's comments about his dealings with the guilds one finds an awareness of his audience's needs that redounds to the dramatist's credit.

Perhaps such a sensitivity helped assure regular employment in the
Lord Mayor's Shows of the 1630s.

Heywood's knowledge of masques and antimasques becomes apparent
in his 1634 play Love's Mistress, or The Queen's Masque, which within
"a period of eight days . . . was performed three times before
Charles and Henrietta Maria--first at a private dress-rehearsal at
the Phoenix, and twice again at Denmark House."[6] Even Inigo Jones
assisted. But it is misleading, I think, to classify this play as a
masque, as some have done. It is, after all, a full-fledged, five-
act play, admittedly with masque elements. Harbage and Schoenbaum in
the Annals of English Drama opt to classify it as "classical legend."
What has received very little critical attention is the fragmentary
masque that I include in this edition of Heywood's entertainments.

Located in Heywood's Pleasant Dialogues and Drammas (1637), the
masque, presumably performed in January 1637, took place at the
residence of Henry Carey, Earl of Dover and Baron of Hunsdon, and
grandson of Queen Elizabeth's kinsman and Lord Chamberlain. In fact,
Heywood dedicates the whole volume of Pleasant Dialogues to Carey.
What little remains of the masque is mainly classical and
mythological in its focus. But it offers testimony to something else
new that Heywood attempted in the 1630s: the masque. Thus in the
dramatic form of pageantry, Heywood explores all forms in this final
decade of his dramatic career.

I turn finally to a consideration of Heywood's subject matter in
the pageants. Given Heywood's career as a writer up to the 1630s in
which he had explored just about every literary form and pursued a
wide variety of topics, one understands the range of Heywood's
thematic material in the pageants. In this he resembles several
other pageant writers. As I suggested in my chapter on Heywood
several years ago, Heywood demonstrates here and elsewhere a high
level of knowledge of classical writers and subjects; indeed, Heywood
as classicist remains a topic to be fully explored. A partial list
of ancient writers quoted or referred to in the pageants includes
Ovid, Horace, Tacitus, Livy, Seneca, Varo, Plutarch, Pythagoras,
Pliny, Cato, Claudian, Aristotle, Plato, Socrates, Plautus, Lucan,
Cicero, Epictetus, Xenophon, Eutropius, and Laberius. Mythological
figures abound in the pageants, such as Ulysses, Arion, Andromeda,
Perseus, Mercury, Juno, Pallas, Venus, Mars, Bellona, Proteus, Janus,
and Orpheus. In the use of such writers and mythological figures
Heywood differs only in degree from other pageant dramatists.

I want instead to focus on Heywood as a moral and religious
writer. This may not seem particularly new since Clark argued years
ago for Heywood's "Puritanism." Most recently, Baines has assessed
the issue and decided that Heywood was not a card-carrying Puritan
(Thomas Heywood, p. 7). I think that she is correct and that the
application of the label "Puritan" reflects a confusion about what

6

the term means and a habit of designating anything at this point in
the seventeenth century that smacks of moral or religious instruction
as "Puritan." A statement prefixed to an edition of Heywood's
Apology for Actors reveals something of the difficulty; the editor
writes: "His best work is A Woman Killed with Kindness (1603), which
is both a pioneer domestic tragedy and a moving study of Puritan
mores. An Apology for Actors (1612) is a professional playwright's
defense of the theatre against Puritan opposition."[7] One cannot
really have it both ways. Heywood makes it very clear in the Apology
that he vigorously opposes the Puritan attack on the theater; this
alone tends to rule out the prospects of his being a Puritan. But he
is absorbed with religious and moral issues, as is apparent in the
pageants.

Heywood's consistent treatment of religious and Biblical material
sets him apart from most of the pageant writers of the Stuart period;
indeed, his emphasis takes us back to the sixteenth-century Midsummer
Shows, also sponsored by the London guilds and almost exclusively
religious in their content. In doing something seemingly new,
Heywood does something quite old: he restores a religious
perspective largely absent from Stuart street pageants. Signifi-
cantly, Heywood's theological perspective often connects with
political ideas. He presents religious characters, concepts, and
architectural structures that symbolize spiritual bliss. His
interest in such religious matters is also apparent in his The
Hierarchy of the Blessed Angels (1634), a book inspired by medieval
traditions, often indebted to St. Thomas Aquinas even if it is, in
the words of Clark, "a great jungle of fact and fiction, science and
the reverse, superstition and shaky metaphysical" (p. 146).

Heywood is the only pageant writer in the Stuart era regularly to
represent the patron saint of the sponsoring guild in the pageant
itself. Only John Squire before him in the 1620 Lord Mayor's Show,
The Triumphs of Peace, had tried this procedure. Using religious or
Biblical figures in pageants had suffered a major decline after the
Elizabethan period, but Heywood revives the once common feature.
Three times he includes a representation of Saint Catherine of
Alexandria, the patroness of the Haberdashers guild. She offers not
only moral or instructional concepts but also political ideas.

In front of the Palace of Honor in the 1631 pageant, St.
Catherine awaits the mayor's arrival in order to welcome him into
Honor's presence. Heywood offers in the text a brief history of the
saint, noting, for example, that "she lived and dyed a Virgin and a
Martyr under the Tirany of Maxentius, whose Empresse, with many other
great and eminent persons she had before converted to the Faith."
Catherine characterizes herself in her speech as "A queene, a Virgin,
and a Martir" and notes that the wheel she carries is not "Blind
Fortunes Embleame"; instead, "Mine is the Wheele of Faith. . . ." By
adhering to her pattern and seeking the power from which flows all

goodness and virtue, the mayor may achieve "trew Caelestiall
grace. . . ." Her moral instructions to the mayor are explicit and
practical: "To curbe the opressor, the opprest to inlarge;/ To be
the Widdowes Husband, th' Orphants Father,/ The blindmans eye, the
lame mans foot." To follow such a moral and compassionate course
also assures that the mayor will be a sound magistrate, cognizant of
the needs of his people.

When Heywood presented Catherine again in the 1632 show, he
placed her on the back of a lion "bordered about with Sea-waves (the
Armes of the Haberdashers)." Again she carries a wheel, "full of
sharpe cutting Irons, the Embleame of her Martyrdome." Heywood
mentions that in the previous show he had discussed her history and
therefore he proceeds now to her speech. Sounding a bit as if she
has come from The Faerie Queene, Catherine explains why she sits
mounted on a lion: ". . . (being a Queene) this kingly beast doth
owe/ Mee duty by instinct." Her banner contains the motto of the
Haberdashers: serve and obey. Underscoring political order, the
saint observes: ". . . whosoever shall himselfe oppose/ Against this
Magistrate, (as one of those/ The King deputes as Chiefe) himselfe
hee brings/ To bee a rebell to the King of Kings." Like her
predecessor, this Catherine also enumerates virtues that the mayor
should seek. He must somehow avoid any "crosse interposition/
Betwixt Power and Obedience. . . ." In her own way this patron saint
of the guild offers a miniature mirror for magistrates, a blend of
moral and political instruction.

For the final time Heywood in 1637 includes Catherine. One
wonders if for some reason the committee of the Haberdashers
esepcially wanted or required the representation of their patroness.
At any rate, Heywood includes her, this time on the river Thames:
"she rideth on a Scallop, which is part of his Lordships Coate of
Armes, drawne in a Sea-Chariot, by two Sea-horses. . . ." Catherine
speaks at some length, explaining why she appears on water rather
than on land--one may rightly sense an element of strain in Heywood's
imagination at this point. She comes, she says, at Jove's command,
as she recounts a council of the gods to discuss how they may best
celebrate the inauguration of the new mayor. Using, at his request,
two of Neptune's sea-horses, Catherine comes to join in the welcome.
Absent, however, is the usual moral instruction; that comes from
others in the land devices. But by representing Catherine, Heywood
honors the guild, calls attention to its religious heritage, and
underscores the great moral strength of this virgin martyr. The
implications for the new mayor seem clear.

The Biblical concept that Heywood represents in several pageants
is the doctrine of the Theological Graces--Faith, Hope, and Charity--
as found in 1 Corinthians 13:1-13. In the Renaissance imagination
these Graces seem to have been constructed as counters to the popular
mythological Graces. The Theological Graces appear in several Tudor-

Stuart pageants, beginning with George Peele's <u>Descensus</u> <u>Astraeae</u>, the 1591 Lord Mayor's Show. In Peele's entertainment the Theological Graces appear side by side with the other Graces. Heywood places the Biblical Graces in a context that calls attention to politics or government in the kingdom.

The first show on land in the 1631 pageant underscores the qualities needed to assure a well governed city. In addition to Time and Truth, the presiding figure in the device, "a woman of beautifull aspect, apparrelled like Summer," has three attendants, "three Damsels habited according to their qualitie, and representing the three Theological vertues, <u>Faith</u>, <u>Hope</u>, and <u>Charity</u>." Time as interpreter and speaker allies the Theological Graces with the causes for a flourishing commonwealth--all strongly reminiscent of a tableau presented to Queen Elizabeth in her 1559 royal entry into London. The mayor in the 1633 pageant could see the Theological Graces as occupants in the pageant device called the "Bower of Blisse." Here they accompany the four Cardinal Virtues and are, Heywood says, "hand-maides attending to conduct all such pious and religious Magistrates, the way to the caelestiall Bower of Blisse. . . ." These Graces show, in the words of Prudence, the speaker, "the stepps by which to rise" to celestial happiness. One last time in Heywood's pageants the Graces appear in his 1638 show; they are among the occupants of the Gate of Piety. Each virtue has an escutcheon with an appropriate motto: Faith, "<u>The</u> <u>wings</u> <u>of</u> <u>Faith</u> <u>are</u> <u>the</u> <u>ladder</u> <u>by</u> <u>which</u> <u>we</u> <u>scale</u> <u>heaven</u>"; Hope, "<u>hee</u> <u>hates</u> <u>the</u> <u>Earth</u>, <u>that</u> <u>hopes</u> <u>for</u> <u>Heaven</u>"; and Love "<u>who</u> <u>giveth</u> <u>willingly</u>, <u>shall</u> <u>never</u> <u>want</u> <u>wretchedly</u>." Derived from the Bible, these Graces offer the mayor spiritual instruction, thereby commenting on the nature of government and the magistrate's readiness to rule. The presence of the Graces in Heywood's pageants reinforces the pervasive religious subject matter and tone of his mayoral shows.

Heywood further gives such moral and religious ideas a local habitation by devising specific pageant devices or tableaux that emphasize spiritual matters. For example, in the 1633 show Heywood offers the Bower of Bliss, one most unlike Spenser's in <u>The</u> <u>Faerie</u> <u>Queene</u>. Heywood's description is at best general: "a curious and neatly framed Architecture, beautified with many proper and becomming Ornaments." He is more precise about its symbolic importance: "An Embleame of that future Happinesse, which not onely all just and upright Magistrates, but every good man, of what condition or quality soever in the course of his life, especially aimeth at." At some length Heywood explores the significance of the occupants of the Bower: the Cardinal and Theological Virtues. Prudence explains that from this earthly Bower of Bliss the mayor Ralph Freeman may envision the future when he shall "Fin'd and repur'd to all Eternity: / . . . arrive at yon Caelestiall Tower,/ Which aptly may be titled <u>Freemans</u> <u>Bower</u>." The Virtues and Graces shall attend him as he ascends on the "unseene wings" of the Graces.

Eventually he will presumably arrive "Where Saints and Angels Haleluiahs sing"--reminding one, perhaps, of the ending of Everyman.

The last device in the 1635 pageant is called Sinus Salutis, the bosom or harbor of Health and Happiness. Heywood writes: "The sculpture being adorned with eight several persons, representing such vertues as are necessary to bee imbraced by all such Majestrates, who after their stormy and tempestuous progresse . . . seeke to anchor in that safe and secure Port so styled." Heywood offers insight into why he calls so much attention to the spiritual life of the mayor: "Every Magistrate is a minister under God, appointed by his divine ordinance to that calling, to be a protector of the Church, a preserver of discipline and Peace. . . ." This insistently Protestant view explains Heywood's preoccupation with instructing the new mayor in his spiritual life; indeed, for Heywood there can be no separation of the magistrate's spiritual or moral life from his political responsibilities. For Heywood, the mayor's sword is, in the speaker's words, "tutch'd with Truth's Adamant."

Joining such tableaux that underscore moral and religious values is the Porta Pietatis device in the 1638 pageant. This Gate of Piety contains several allegorical figures who represent the qualities the new mayor should have, qualities that determine his ability to govern wisely. Heywood describes the structure briefly: "a delicate and artificiall composed structure, built Temple-fashion, as most genuine and proper to the persons therein presented." The chief figure is Piety; "upon her head are certaine beames or raies of gold, intimating a glory belonging to sanctity; in one hand an Angelical staffe, with a Banner; on the other Arme a Crosse Gules in a field Argent." Several other characters accompany Piety, such as Religion, the Theological Virtues, Zeal, Humility, and Constancy; each has an appropriate emblem and motto.

But perhaps the most startling or unexpected person represented is the Virgin Mary. This pageant honors Maurice Abbot, Draper, himself brother of George Abbot late Archbishop of Canterbury, and of Robert Abbot, once Bishop of Salisbury. Such information, combined with the Drapers' history as the fraternity of the Virgin Mary, presumably led Heywood to write this his most religiously-oriented entertainment. Heywood had elsewhere, as I have shown, represented the patron saint, Catherine, of the Haberdashers; thus in one sense he merely continues that practice. Representing the Virgin, however, in the increasingly Puritan London of the late 1630s challenges conventional expectation. One might consider it bold, in fact.

Heywood describes the Virgin as a companion of Piety: "In another compartment sitteth one representing the blessed Virgin, Patronesse of this Right Worshipfull Society, Crowned: in one hand a Fanne of Starres, in the other a Shield, in which are inscribed three Crownes . . . ascending. . . ." Her motto corresponds to that of the

Drapers: to God only be honor and glory (Deo soli Honor & gloria).
Piety, the speaker, calls attention to the Virgin: "Your Virgin-
Saint sits next Religion crown'd/ With her owne Hand-maids (see)
inviron'd round. . . ." Heywood's presentation of the Virgin seems
to give the lie to Heywood's presumed Puritanism. Her presence in
this pageant is unorthodox because she does not appear elsewhere in
Tudor and Stuart pageants, even in other pageants honoring the
Drapers.

In part her presence encourages Heywood to defend established
religion. Piety says, for example:

> Here sits Religion firme, (though else where torne
> By Schismaticks, and made the Atheists scorne)
> Shining in her pure truth, nor need she quake,
> Affrighted with the Faggot and the stake:
> Shee's to you deare, you unto her are tender,
> Under the Scepter of the Faiths defender.

This defense of the established religion seems hardly a Puritan
speaking. Heywood thus embraces throughout his pageants the theme of
the inseparability of the moral and the political life. More than
other pageant dramatists, Heywood seeks to establish the requisites
of good government by using moral and religious references.

After Heywood's 1639 pageant, we find this ominous record in the
Grocers' Court Books for 1640: "their is noe publike show eyther wth
Pageats or vppon the water" (Malone Society, Collections III, p.
131). Soon the voices of all dramatists will be silenced and the
theaters closed. With the advent of civil strife, street pageants
could no longer survive. Curiously, Heywood emphasizes in an
uncanny, prescient way the struggle between war and peace in his last
pageant--the last word in the street entertainments until the
Restoration. Heywood's voice cries out for a peaceful and moral
government, but the swirling forces of enmity and war drown such
pleas. In the face of war, pageants indeed become insubstantial.

This edition provides a critical, old-spelling text of the
pageants of Thomas Heywood. Textual problems in these pageants are
relatively slight. All of Heywood's texts exist in only one edition,
though the 1632 pageant, Londini Artium, has two different issues.
All texts were printed by the Okes print shop, except for the 1635
one, Londini Sinus Salutis, which was printed by Robert Raworth and
is the only one to be in octavo form. Such textual problems as exist
will be discussed at the end of each pageant text.

Evidence of press correction is limited--not surprising given the
nature of the texts, usually printed hurriedly for the occasion of

the pageant or shortly thereafter. One interesting case, however, is the 1631 text, <u>Londons Jus Honorarium</u>, where, as I demonstrate, we find evidence of two compositors having set the type for this quarto. This is quite rare. All press variants are recorded in the "Collation" section following the pageants. For this edition all of the extant quarto and octavo copies have been examined, as well as any later reprints, such as the 1874 Heywood edition. Any significant differences have been recorded in the Collation.

I think it reasonable to assume that the manuscripts which served as printer's copy for the pamphlets were probably Heywood's foul papers or fair copies. The usual problem of textual transmission, as we find with most play quartos, is not a consideration with these pageants, there being, of course, no theatrical transmission and only one edition. Considering the intimate relationship between pageant-dramatist, guild and the printer, it seems likely that Heywood would send his own manuscript to the printer. He refers in one of the texts to his "unperfect" papers.

I have attempted to preserve faithfully the accidentals of the copy-text; thus the spelling is changed only when it is obvious that the compositor has made an error. My approach to punctuation has also been conservative; I have emended the pointing only when change was patently needed, such as in the failure to have terminal punctuation for a sentence or when the pointing is too strong and interrupts or interferes with the reading. Thus the alterations in the accidentals have been few, and they are duly recorded. Elizabethan syntax and punctuation are not modern syntax and punctuation, Heywood and others having little of our sense of subordination. I have thought it best not to tamper much with this problem. I have lightened the punctuation occasionally when the sentences were particularly vexing because of the heavy pointing.

The texts have been silently emended in several areas. I have, for example, consistently changed the <u>u-v</u> and <u>i-j</u> to reflect modern practice. When there are obvious errors in capitalization, I have emended silently. Most abbreviations, ampersands, and words which have a tilde for a nasal have been silently expanded. No attempt has been made to reproduce all the typographical features of the pamphlets. All of the italic type, for example, has not been preserved, for there is no consistent pattern in the quartos.

Following the text of each pageant there is a section called "Textual Notes," which begins with a brief introduction of what is known about the quarto or octavo and where extant copies are located. The collation of these copies and the press variants are recorded in the section on "Collation." I also include here the comparison with later reprints, as well as any emendations. The reading of this edition will be found to the left of the square bracket in the collation.

12

Notes

[1]A. M. Clark, <u>Thomas Heywood</u>: <u>Playwright</u> <u>and</u> <u>Miscellanist</u> (Oxford: Basil Blackwell, 1931), p. 117.

[2]Frederick S. Boas, <u>Thomas Heywood</u> (London: Williams & Norgate, 1950), pp. 147-153.

[3]Michel Grivelet, <u>Thomas Heywood et le drame domestique élizabéthain</u> (Paris: Didier, 1957), pp. 87-88.

[4]Barbara J. Baines, <u>Thomas Heywood</u> (Boston: Twayne, 1984), p. 147.

[5]See my <u>English Civic Pageantry 1558-1642</u> (London: Arnold; Columbia: Univ. of South Carolina, 1971), pp. 217-241.

[6]Raymond C. Shady, "Thomas Heywood's Masque at Court," in <u>Elizabethan Theatre VII</u>, ed. G. R. Hibbard (Hamden, CT: Archon, 1980), p. 147. Shady's fine discussion appears on pp. 147-166.

[7]O. B. Hardison, Jr., ed. <u>English Literary Critcism</u>: <u>The Renaissance</u> (New York: Appleton-Century-Crofts, 1963), p. 221.

Londons Jus Honorarium.

Exprest in sundry triumphs, pagiants, and shews:
At the Initiation or Entrance of the Right Honourable
George Whitmore, into the Maioralty of the famous and
farre renouned City of London.

All the charge and expence of the laborious projects, and objects both by Water and Land, being the
sole undertaking of the Right Worshipfull, the
Society of the Habberdashers.
Redeunt Spectacula.

Printed at London by NICHOLAS OKES. 1631.

Londons Ius Honorarium.

Exprest in sundry Triumphs, pagiants, and shews:
At the Initiation or Entrance of the Right Honourable
George Whitmore, into the Maioralty of the famous and
farrerenouned City of *London*.

All the charge and expence of the laborious proiects, and obiects both by Water and Land, being the
sole vndertaking of the Right Worshipfull, the
society of the *Habburdashers*.
Redeunt spectacula.

Printed at *London* by NICHOLAS OKES. 1631.

Title page of *Londons Jus Honorarium* (1631). Reproduced by
permission of the Huntington Library, San Marino, California.

15

To the Right Honourable, George
Whitmore, Lord Maior of this renowned
Metropolis, London.

Right Honorable,

   It was the speech of a Learned and grave Philosopher the Tutor
and Counseler to the Emperour Gratianus, Pulcrius multo parari, quam
creari nobilem. More faire and famous it is to be made, then to be
borne Noble, for that Honour is to be most Honored, which is purchast
by merrit, not crept into by descent: For you whose goodnesse, hath
made you thus great, I make my affectionate presentment of this   10
annuall Celebration, concerning which (without flattery be it spoken)
there is nothing so much as mentioned (much lesse enforced) in this
your Jus honorarium, which rather commeth not short, then anyway
exceedeth the hope and expectation which is now upon you; and
therefore worthily was your so free Election, without either
emulation, or competitorship conferd upon you; since of you it may be
undeniably spoken: that none ever in your place was more sufficient
or able, any cause whatsoever shall be brought before you, more truly
to discerne; being apprehended more advisedly to dispose, being
digested, more maturely to despatch. After this short tender of my   20
service unto you, I humbly take my leave, with this sentence borrowed
from Seneca: Decet timeri Magistratum, at plus diligi.

                    Your Lordships in all
                       observance,

                    Thomas Heywood.

16

To the Right Worshipfull Samuell
Cranmer, and Henry Pratt, the two
Sheriffs of the Honourable Citty of
London, Lately Elected.

Right Worshipfull,   30

The cheife Magistrats next unto the Lord Maior, are the two
sheriffes, the name Sheriffe implyeth as much as the Reeve and
Governour of a Sheire, for Reeve is Grave Count or Earle (for so
saith Master Verstigan): and these, were of like authority with the
Censors, who were reputed in the prime and best ranke amongst the
Magistrates of Rome. They were so cal'd a Cessendo, of ceasing, for
they set a rate upon every mans estate: registring their names, and
placing them in a fit century: A second part of their Office
consisted in the reforming of maners, as having power to inquire into
every mans life and carriage. The Embleame of which Authority was   40
their Tirgula censoria borne before them: they are (by others)
resembled to the Tribunes of the people, and these are cal'd Sacro
Sancti, whose persons might not be injured, nor their names any way
scandaliz'd, for whosoever was proved to be a delinquent in either,
was held to be Homo sacer; an excommunicated person, and hee that
slew him was not liable unto any Judgement: their Houses stand open
continually, not onely for Hospitality, but for a Sanctuary to all
such as were distrest: neither was it lawfull for them to be absent
from the Colledge one whole day together, during their Yeare. Thus
you see how neere the Dignities of this Citty, come neere to these in   50
Rome, when it was most flourishing. The first Sheriffes that bore
the name and office in this Citty, were Peter Duke, and Thomas Neale,
Anno 1209. The novissimi, now in present Samuell Cranmer and Henry
Pratt, Anno 1631. To whom I direct this short Remembrance.

                    Your Worships ever
                    Attendant,

                    Thomas Heywood.

L O N D O N S
JUS HONORARIUM.

When Rome was erected at the first establishing of a common
weale, Romulus the founder of it, instituted a prime officer to
governe the Citty, who was cald praefectus urbis, i. the praefect of
the City, whose uncontroulable authority, had power, not onely to
examine, but to determine, all causes and controversies, and to sit
upon, and censure all delinquents, whether their offences were
capitall or criminall: Intra centessimum lapidem, within an hundred
miles of the City, in processe of time the Tarquins being expeld, and
the prime soveraignty remaining in the consuls. They (by reason of
their forraigne imployments) having no leasure to administer Justice
at home, created two cheife officers, the one they cald praetor
urbanus, or Maior, the other peregrinus: The first had his
jurisdiction, in and over the Citty, the other excercised his
authority meerely upon strangers.

The name Praetor is derived from Praeessendo or Praeeundo, from
priority of place, which as a learned Roman Author writs, had
absolute power over all publique and privat affaires, to make new
Lawes, and abolish old, without controwle, or contradiction: His
authority growing to that height, that whatsoever he decreed or
censured in publique, was cald Jus Honorarium, the first on whome
this dignity was conferd in Rome, was spurius furius Camillus, the
sonne of Marcus: And the first Praetor or Lord Maior appointed to
the Government of the Honorable Citty of London, was Henry Fitz
Allwin, advaunced to that Dignity, by King John, Anno 1210. So much
for the Honor and Antiquity of the name and place. I proceede to the
showes.

Upon the water.

Are two craggy Rockes, plac'd directly opposit, of that distance
that the Barges may passe betwixt them: these are full of monsters,
as Serpents, Snakes, Dragons, &c. some spitting Fier, others vomiting
water; in the bases thereof, nothing to be seene, but the sad relicks
of shipwracke in broken Barkes and split Vessels, &c. The one is
cald Silla, the other Charibdis, which is scituate directly against
Messana; Scilla against Rhegium: and whatsoever shippe that passeth
these Seas, if it keepe not the middle Channell, it is either wrackt
upon the one, or devoured by the other; Medio tutissimus ibit. Upon
these Rocks are placed the Syrens, excellent both in voyce and
Instrument: They are three in number, Telsipio, Iligi, Aglaosi: or
as others will have them called, Parthenope, skilfull in musicke;
Leucosia, upon the winde Instrument; Ligni, upon the Harpe. The

60

70

80

90

18

morrall intended by the Poets, that whosoever shall lend an attentive   100
eare to their musicke, is in great danger to perish; but he that can
warily avoyd it by stopping his eares against their inchantment,
shall not onely secure themselves, but bee their ruine: This was
made good in Ulisses the speaker, who by his wisedome and pollicy not
onely preserved himselfe and his people, but was the cause that they
from the rocks cast themselves headlong into the Sea. In him is
personated a wise and discreete Magistrate.

                    Ulisses his speech.

    Behold great Magistrate, on either hand
Sands, Shelves, and Syrtes, and upon them stand   110
Two dangerous rocks, your safety to ingage,
Boasting of nought save shipwrake spoyle and strage.
This Sylla, that Charibdis, (dangerous both)
Plac't in the way you rowe to take your oath.

    Yet though a thousand monsters yawne and gape
To ingurdge and swallow you, ther's a way to scape;
Ulisses by his wisedome found it, steare
You by his Compasse, and the way lyes cleare,
Will you know how? looke upward then; and sayle
By the signe Libra, that Celestiall scale,   120
In which (some write) the Sunne at his creation
First shone; and is to these times a relation
Of Divine Justice: It, in justice shind,
Doe you so (Lord) and be like it divind.

    Keepe the even Channell, and be neither swayde,
To the right hand nor left, and so evade
Malicious envie (never out of action,)
Smooth visadgd flattery, and blackemouthd detraction,
Sedition, whisprings, murmuring, private hate,
All ambushing the godlike Magistrate.   130

    About these rockes and quicksands Syrens haunt,
One singes connivence, th' other would inchaunt
With partiall sentence; and a third ascribes,
In pleasing tunes, a right to gifts and bribes;
Sweetning the eare, and every other sence,
That place, and office, may with these dispence.
But though their tones be sweete, and shrill their notes,
They come from foule brests, and impostum'd throats,
Sea monsters they be stiled, but much (nay more,
'Tis to be doubted,) they frequent the shoare.   140

       Yet like Ulisses, doe but stop your eare
To their inchantments, with an heart sincere;
They fayling to indanger your estate,
Will from the rocks themselves precipitate.

       Proceede then in your blest Inauguration,
And celebrate this Annuall Ovation;
Whilst you nor this way, nor to that way leane,
But shunne th' extreames, to keepe the golden meane.
This glorious City, Europs chiefest minion,   150
Most happy in so great a Kings dominion:
Into whose charge this day doth you invest,
Shall her in you, and you in her make blest.

       The first show by Land, (presented in Pauls Churchyard), is a   The first show
greene and pleasant Hill, adorned with all the Flowers of the spring,   by land.
upon which is erected a faire and flourishing tree, furnished with
variety of faire and pleasant fruite, under which tree, and in the
most eminent place of the Hill, sitteth a woman of beautifull aspect,
apparrelled like Summer: Her motto, Civitas bene Gubernata, i. a
City well governed. Her Attendants (or rather Associats) are three
Damsels habited according to their qualitie, and representing the   160
three Theologicall vertues, Faith, Hope, and Charity: Amongst the
leaves and fruits of this Tree, are inserted diverse labels with
severall sentences expressing the causes which make Cities to
flourish and prosper: As, The feare of God, Religious zeale, A Wise
Magistrate, Obedience to rulers, Unity, Plaine and faithfull dealing,
with others of the like nature. At the foot of the Hill sitteth old
Time, and by him his daughter Truth, with this inscription; Veritas
est Temporis Filia, i. Truth is the Daughter of Time: which Time   Tymes speech
speaketh as followeth.
                                                                       Non nova sunt
                                                                       semper, &
                                                                       quod fuit An-
       If Time (some say) have here bin oft in view,   te relictum
Yet not the same, old Time is each day new,   est sit que
Who doth the future lockt up houres inlarge,   quod haud
To welcome you to this great Cities charge.   fuerat, &c.
Time, who hath brought you hither (grave and great)
To inaugure you, in your Praetorium seate:
Thus much with griefe doth of himselfe professe
Nothing's more precious, and esteemed lesse.
Yet you have made great use of me, to aspire
This eminence, by desert, when in full quire
Avees and Acclamations, with loud voyce,   180
Meete you on all sides, and with Time rejoyce.

       This Hill, that Nimph apparreld like the Spring,
These Graces that attend her, (every thing)
As fruitfull trees, greene plants, flowers of choise smell,

All Emblems of a City governd well;
Which must be now your charge. The Labels here
Mixt with the leaves will shew what fruit they beare:
The feare of God, a Magistrate discreete,
Justice, and Equity: when with these meete,
Obedience unto Rulers, Unity,   190
Plaine and just dealing, Zeale, and Industry:
In such blest symptoms where these shall agree,
Cities, shall like perpetuall Summers bee.

       You are now Generall, doe but bravely lead,
And (doubtlesse) all will march, as you shall tread:
You are the Captaine, doe but bravely stand
To oppose vice, see all this goodly band
Now in their City Liveries will apply
Themselves to follow, where your Colours fly.
You are the chiefe, defend my daughter Truth,   200
And then both Health and Poverty, Age and Youth,
Will follow this your Standard, to oppose
Errour, Sedition, Hate, (the common foes).

       But pardon Time (grave Lord) who speaks to thee;
As well what thou now art, as ought to be.

       Then Time maketh a pause, and taking up a leafelesse and withered
branch, thus proceedeth.

       See you this withered branch, by Time o're growne
A Cities Symbole, ruind, and trod downe.
A Tree that bare bad fruit; Dissimulation,   210
Pride, Malice, Envy, Atheisme, Supplantation,
Ill Government, Prophannes, Fraud, Oppression,
Neglect of vertue, Freedome to transgression,
Disobedience, here with power did disagree
All which faire London be still farre from thee.

       The second show by Land, is presented in the upper part of   The second show
Cheapside, which is a Chariot; the two beasts that are placed before   by land.
it, are a Lyon passant, and a white Unicorne in the same posture, on
whose backs are seated two Ladies, the one representing Justice upon
the Lyon, the other Mercy upon the Unicorne. The motto which Justice   220
beareth, is Rebelles protero; the inscription which Mercy carrieth,
is Imbelles protego: Herein is intimated, that by these types and
symboles of Honour (represented in these noble beasts belonging to
his Majestie) all other inferiour magistracies and governments either
in Common weales, or private Societies, receive both being and
supportance.

The prime Lady seated in the first and most eminent place of the Chariot, representeth London, behinde whom, and on either side, diverse others of the chiefe Cities of the Kingdome take place: As Westminster, Yorke, Bristoll, Oxford, Lincolne, Exeter, &c. All these are to be distinguished by their severall Escutchons; to them London being Speaker, directeth the first part of her speech as followeth.

230

You noble Citties of this generous Isle,
May these my two Coacht Ladies ever smile
(Justice, and mercy) on you. You we know
Are come to grace this our triumphant show.
And of your curtesy, the hand to kisse
Of London, this faire lands Metropolis.

London the
speaker.

Why sister Cittyes sit you thus amazd?
Ist to behold about you, windowes glas'd
With Diomonds 'sted of glasse? Starres hither sent,
This day to deck our lower Firmament?

240

Is it to see my numerous Children round
Incompasse me? So that no place is found
In all my large streets empty? My yssue spred
In number more then stones whereon they tread.
To see my Temples, Houses, even all places
With people covered, as if tyl'd with faces?

Will you know whence proceedes this faire increase,
This joy? the fruits of a continued peace,
The way to thrive; to prosper in each calling,
The weake, and shrinking states, to keepe from falling,
Behold my motto shall all this display,
Reade and observe it well: Serve and obay.
Obedience through it humbly doth begin,
It soone augments unto a Magozin
Of plenty, in all Citties 'tis the grownd,
And doth like harmony in musicke sound:
Nations and Common weales, by it alone
Flourish: It incorporates, many into one
And makes unanimous peace content and joy,
Which pride, doth still insidiate to destroy.

250

Serve and
obey: the
Motto of the
Worshipfull
Company of
the Habber-
dashers

And you grave Lord, on whom right honour cals,
Both borne and bred i' th' circuit of my wals,
By vertue and example, have made plaine,
How others may like eminence attaine.

Persist in this blest concord, may we long,
That Citties to this City may still throng,

To view my annuall tryumphs, and so grace,   270
Those honored <u>Pretors</u> that supply this place.

    Next after the Chariot, are borne the two rocks, <u>Sylla</u> and
<u>Caribdis</u>, which before were presented upon the water: upon the top
of the one stands a Sea Lyon, upon the other a Meare-maide or <u>Sea-</u>
<u>Nimphe</u>, the <u>Sirens</u> and <u>Monsters</u>, beeing in continuall agitation and
motion, some breathing fire, others spowting water. I shall not
neede to spend much time in the description of them, the worke being
sufficiently able to commend itselfe.

    The third shew by Land presented neere unto the great Crosse in
Cheape-side, beareth the title of the <u>Palace of Honour</u>: A faire and   280
Curious structure archt and Tarrest above, on the Top of which
standeth <u>Honour</u>, a Glorious presens, and ritchly habited, shee in her
speech directed to the right Honorable the Lord Maior, discovers all
the true and direct wayes to attaine unto her as, first: A King:
Eyther by succession or Election. A Souldier, by valour and martiall
Discipline. A Churchman by Learning and degrees in scooles. A
Statesman by Travell and Language &c. A Lord Maior by Commerce and
Trafficke both by Sea and Land, by the Inriching of the Kingdome, and
Honour of our Nation. The Palace of Honour is thus governed

    Industry <u>Controwler</u>, his Word <u>Negotior</u>.   290
    Charity <u>Steward</u>, the Word <u>Miserior</u>.
    Liberality <u>Treasurer</u>, the Word <u>Largior</u>.
    <u>Innocence</u> and <u>Devotion</u>, <u>Henchmen</u> the words,
    <u>Patior</u>: <u>Precor</u>.

And so of the rest, and according to this Pallace of <u>Honour</u> is
facioned not onely the management of the whole <u>Citty</u> in generall:
but the House and Family of the <u>Lord Maior</u> in particuler.

    Before in the front of this pallace is seated Saint <u>Katherin</u>, the
Lady and Patronesse of this Worshipfull Society of whom I will give
you this short Character. The name it selfe imports in the   300
Originall: <u>Omnis</u> <u>ruina</u>, which (as some interpret it) is as much as
to say, the fall and ruin of all the workes of the Divell: Others
derive the word from <u>Catena</u>, a Chaine wherein all cheife Vertues and
Graces are concatinated and link't together; so much for her name.

    For her birth, shee was lineally descended from the Roman
Emperours, the daughter of <u>Costus</u> the sonne of <u>Constantine</u> which
<u>Costus</u> was crowned King of <u>Armenia</u>, for <u>Constantine</u> having conquered
that Kingdome, grew Inamored of the Kings Daughter by whom he had
Issue, this <u>Costus</u> who after succeeded his Grand Father.

Constantine after the death of his first Wife made an expedition   310
from Roome, and having Conquered this Kingdome of Great Britaine, he
tooke to his Second Wife Helena, which Helena was she that found the
Crosse upon which the Saviour of the World was Crucified, &c.

Costus dying whilst Katherine was yet young, and shee being all
that time living in Famogosta, (a cheife City, because shee was there
Proclaimed and Crowned and called Queene of Famogosta), she lived and
dyed a Virgin and a Martyr under the Tiranny of Maxentius, whose
Empresse, with many other great and eminent persons she had before
converted to the Faith. So much for her character. Her speech to
the Lord Maior as followeth.   320

I Katherin, long since Sainted for true piety,
The Lady patronesse of this Society,
A queene, a Virgin, and a Martir: All
My Atributes invite you to this Hall
Cald Honours pallace: nor is this my Wheele,
Blind Fortunes Embleame, she that makes to reele
Kingdomes and Common weales, all turning round,
Some to advance, and others to Confound:

Mine is the Wheele of Faith, (all wayes in motion)
Stedfast in Hope, and Constant in Devotion.   330
It imitates the Spheres swift agitation,
Orbicularly, still moving to Salvation:
That's to the Primus motor: from whom Flowes,
All Goodnesse, Vertue: There, true Honour growes,
Which if you will attaine 't must be your care,
(Grave Magistrate), Instated as you are
To keepe this Curcular action, in your charge,
To curbe the opressor, the opprest to inlarge;
To be the Widdowes Husband, th' Orphants Father,
The blindmans eye, the lame mans foot: so gather   340
A treasure beyond valew, by your place;
(More then Earths Honour), trew Caelestiall grace,
Ayme first at that: what others Honors be,
Honour Her selfe can best Instruct thats shee.

At that word she poynteth upward to a Glorious presens which
personates Honor in the top of the pallace, who thus secondeth Saint
Katherens Speech.

24

Honours Speech.

The way to me though not debard,
Yet it is dificult and hard.   350
If Kings arrive to my profection
Tis by Succession, or Election
When Fortitude doth Action grace,
The Souldier then with me takes place
When Stooddy, Knowledge and degree
Makes Scollers Eminent heere with mee;
They are lifted with the Honored: and
The Travilar, when many a land
He hath peirst for language, and much knowes
A great respected statesman growes.   360

So you, and such as you (Grave Lord)
Who weare this Scarlet, use that Swoord
Collar, and Cap of Maintenance.
These are no things, that come by chance
Or got by sleeping but averse
From these I am gaind: by care, Commerce,
The hazarding of Goods, and men
To Pyrats Rocks, shelves, Tempest, when?
You through a Wildernesse of Seas,
Dangers of wrack, Surprise, Desease   370
Make new descoveryes, for a lasting story
Of this our Kingdomes fame and Nations glory
Thus is that Collar, and your Scarlet worne,
And for such cause, the Sworde before you Borne.
They are the emblems of your Power, and heere
Though curb'd within the Limmet of one yeare,
Yet manadge as they ought by your Indevour
Shall make your name (as new) Honored for ever
Unto which Pallace of peace, rest and blisse,
Supply of all things, where nought wanting is   380
Would these that shall succeede you know the way?
Tis plaine, God, the King Serve and Obay.

I cannot heare forget that in the presentment of my papers to the
Master, Wardens, and Committies of this Right Worshipfull Company of
the Haberdashers (at whose sole expence and charges all the publick
Triumphes of this dayes Solemnity both by water and land, were
Celebrated) nothing here devised or expressed was any way forraigne
unto them, but of all these my conceptions, they were as able to
Judge, as ready to Heare, and to direct as well as to Censure;
neither was there any dificulty which needed a comment, but as soone   390
known as showne, and apprehended as read: which makes me now
confident of the best ranke of the Cittisens: That as to the Honour

and strength both of the Citty and Kingdome in generall, they
excercise Armes in publicke, so to the benefit of their Judgements,
and inriching of their knowledge, they neglect not the studdy of
arts, and practise of literature in private, so that of them it may
be truly said they are, Tam Mercurio quam Marte periti: I proceede
now to the last Speech at night in which Ulisses at the taking leave
of his Lordship at his Gate, useth this short Commemoration, of all
that hath bin included in the former pageants, poynting to them in   400
order, the manner thereof thus.

    Night growes, inviting you to rest, prepare
To rise tomorrow to a whole Yeares care,
Envy still waites on Honour, then provide
Ulisses Wisdome may be still your guide
To stere you through all dangers: Husband Time
That this day brings you to a place sublime,
By the Supporture of his daughter Truth
This Ancient Citty in her pristine Youth,
Your sword may reestablish: and so bring   410
Her still to florish; like that lasting Spring
That London in whose Circuit you were bred
And borne therein, to be the Cheife and Head
Drawne by these two beasts in an Equall line
May in your Mercy and your Justice shine.
So Honour who this day did you Invite
Unto Her palace bids you thus Good Night,
No following day but adde to your Renowne
And this your Charge, with numerous Blessings crowne.

    I have forborne to spend much paper in needelesse and impertinent   420
deciphering the worke, or explaining the habits of the persons, as
being freely exposed to the publicke view of all the Spectators. The
maine show, being performed by the most excellent in that kind, Mr.
Gerard Christmas, who hath exprest his Modals to be exquisite, as
having spared neither Cost nor care, either in the Figures or
ornaments. I shall not neede to point unto them to say, this is a
Lyon, and that an Unicorne, &c. For of this Artist, I may bouldly
and freely thus much speake, though many about the towne may envie
their worke, yet with all their indevor they shall not be able to
compare with their worth. I conclude with Plautus in sticho: Nam   430
curiosus est nemo qui non sit malevolus.

FINIS.

Textual Notes

The extant copies of <u>Londons</u> <u>Jus</u> <u>Honorarium</u> (Greg, <u>Bibliography</u>, no. 448; STC 13351) are found in the Huntington, Yale, Bodleian, and Harvard University libraries. All have been collated in preparing this edition; the press variants are recorded below in the Collation. The variants indicate considerable attention to sheet B with two rounds of correction.

Despite its brevity, the quarto text contains evidence of two compositors having set the type: one sets sheets A and C, and the other, sheet B. The running titles and other spelling peculiarities constitute the evidence. In sheet B the compositor prefers to use swash italic for capital <u>I</u>, while sheet C contains regular italic <u>I</u> throughout. The spelling of the word "chief" is <u>cheife</u> in sheets <u>A</u> and C, and <u>chiefe</u> in B. The most compelling evidence is the use of <u>u</u> and <u>v</u>. Generally, the compositor setting sheets A and C follows the traditional pattern of using initial <u>v</u> for <u>u</u> and medial <u>u</u> for <u>v</u>, but the one responsible for B follows our modern practice of <u>u-v</u> usage. I examine the evidence more fully in my article, "Two Compositors in Heywood's <u>Londons</u> <u>Ius</u> <u>Honorarium</u> (1631)," <u>Studies</u> <u>in</u> <u>Bibliography</u>, 22 (1969), 223-26. I also suggest that sheet B may have been set by an apprentice in Nicholas Okes's shop.

I have also collated the quarto text against the edition of the pageant found in volume 4 of Shepherd's 1874 edition and note the significant changes. I do not record all of Shepherd's spelling or punctuation alterations. The editor of this only modern edition of the pageant seems to have had access to the copy that eventually found its way into the Huntington Library collection.

Collation

(title page) Habberdashers] Habburdashers Q, 1874

  3 Metropolis] Metrapolis Q, 1874

 36 <u>Rome</u>.] <u>Rome</u>? Q

 63 uncontroulable] 1874; unconroulable Q

 64 determine] 1874; determie Q

 81 <u>Praetor</u>] 1874; <u>Praeter</u> Q

 94 if] it 1874

116 ther's a way] Harvard, Yale, Bodleian; ther's way
    Huntington (1874)

123 It,] Harvard, Yale, Bodleian; It Huntington (1874)

138 impostum'd] 1874; inpostum'd Q

170 here bin] bin here 1874

185 of] 1874; af Q

206 leafelesse] Harvard, Yale, Bodleian; leavelesse
    Huntington (1874)

214 Disobedience] Obedience Q, 1874

223 to] 1874; io Q

232 the] he 1874

235 Coacht] Harvard, Yale, Bodleian; each Huntington (1874)

235 smile] smile. Q, 1874

238 kisse] kiste 1874

241 Ist to behold about] Harvard, Yale, Bodleian; If to
    behold above Huntington; Ist to behold above 1874

245 found] found. Q, 1874

248 places] places. Q; places, 1874

263 destroy] Harvard, Bodleian (1874); destrsy Yale,
    Huntington

265 th'] th Q, 1874

277 worke] 1874; wroke Q

316 Crowned and] Crowned was Q, 1874

335 't] t' Q, 1874

337 Curcular] Harvard, Yale, Bodleian; Curoular Huntington
    (1874)

338 the] the' Q, 1874

359 hath peirst] hath' peir'st Q; hath' peirst 1874

28

364 come] 1874; comc Q

378 ever] 1874; ev r Q

390 neither] nether Q, 1874

400 bin] been 1874

403 tomorrow] 1874; to morrrw Q

414 these] 1874; thesc Q

420 impertinent] Inpertinent Q, 1874

423-25 Mr. Gerard Christmas, who hath exprest his Modals to be
         exquisite, as having spared neither] Harvard, Yale,
         Bodleian; Miaster Gerard Christmas hath exprest hia Modals
         to bee exquisite (as having spared nei-ther Huntington
         (1874)

Commentary Notes

This first pageant written by Heywood and honoring the
installation of Sir George Whitmore, Haberdasher, as the new Lord
Mayor, cost the guild some £793. 16s. 4d (Malone Society, Collections
III, p. 121).8 Two items in the guild's disbursement are quite
interesting. First, the Haberdashers paid £2 for the printing of 300
copies of the text; the usual number of copies printed for mayoral
pageants had become 500. Also, a payment of £200 is made to Gerard
Christmas, the artificer, rather than to Heywood. No separate
payment is recorded to Heywood. Such evidence may point to the
increasing importance of the artificer in the 1630s. Obviously
Heywood would be paid for writing the show, but the guild records do
not show how much. Heywood praises both the guild for their
cooperation and Christmas for his artistry in the text.

1 George Whitmore] sheriff 1621, Lord Mayor 1631, knighted
   1632; twice master of the company of the Haberdashers;
   Alderman Farringdon Within and Langbourn; died December
   1654.

5-6 Learned and grave Philosopher the Tutor and Counselor to
     the Emperour Gratianus] St. Ambrose, whom Gratian asked
     to write De Fido.

22 Seneca: Decet timeri Magistratum, at plus diligi] "A
    teacher ought to be feared, but even more, to be loved."

Heywood credits Seneca, but the quotation is not from Seneca.

27 Samuell Cranmer, and Henry Pratt] Cranmer, sheriff 1631, Alderman of Cripplegate; born c. 1575, died 1640; Brewer; related to Archbishop Cranmer. Pratt, sheriff 1631, Merchant Taylor; alderman for Bridge Ward; created Baronet 1641; died 1647.

34 saith Master Verstigan] alias for Richard Rowlands who published under his pseudonym A Restitution of Decayed Intelligence in Antiquities (Antwerp, 1605) in which he discusses the meanings of the titles in Chapter 10; and the particular point Heywood mentions is found on p. 326.

80 furius Camillus, the sonne of Marcus] Marcus Furius Camillus, Roman soldier and statesman, of patrician descent, censor in 403 B.C.; was honored with the title of second founder of Rome.

82 Henry Fitz Allwin] reputedly the first mayor of London, starting in 1190; was mayor until his death in 1212. A person much discussed in Anthony Munday's pageants; see, for example, Munday's Himatia-Poleos, (1614), where he is represented as a character.

92 cald Silla, the other Charibdis] cf. the treatment of these two in Heywood's Gunaikeion: or, Nine Books of Various History Concerninge Women (London, 1624), p. 42, where Heywood insists that "No man but in the progress of his life sailes betwixt these two quicksands"; then Heywood relates them to Aristotle's Ethics and the doctrine of the mean which is borne out in the pageant text in l. 95, Medio tutissimus ibit: "a middle course will be safest."

97 three in number, Telsipio, Iligi, Aglaosi] again cf. the treatment of the Syrens in Heywood's Gunaikeion, pp. 364-5, where Heywood makes a similar moral interpretation as in the pageant.

110 Syrtes] quicksand (OED).

112 strage] slaughter (OED); the first use is cited from a text in 1632--obviously Heywood precedes that.

158 i.] early abbreviation for i.e., id est; this edition retains this form.

166-67 At the foot of the Hill sitteth old Time, and by him his daughter Truth] Heywood's linking of these two and the

whole scene at this point are strongly reminiscent of a
tableau presented in the civic pageant offered to Queen
Elizabeth on her official royal entry into London on 14
January 1559. For a comparison of these two pageants see my
"Symbolic Landscape in English Civic Pageantry," Renaissance
Quarterly, 22 (1969), 32-7. (See also Sheila Williams, "Two
Seventeenth Century Semi-Dramatic Allegories of Truth the
Daughter of Time," Guildhall Miscellany, 2 (1963), 207-220.)
Heywood obviously knew the 1559 pageant if one may judge by
his Englands Elizabeth Her Life and Troubles, p. 227f
(published the year of this Lord Mayor's Show) or his
earlier If You Know Not Me, the closing of Part I, which
duplicates some of the events of the 1559 pageant.

168 (margin) Non nova . . . fuerat] "They are not always
     new, and what was previously has been abandoned and that may
     be which was not."

214 Disobedience] though the quarto copies read Obedience,
     the negative concept of disobedience is what makes sense in
     the catalogue of qualities that destroy a city.

218 a Lyon passant, and a white Unicorne] these are included
     because Heywood apparently associates the animals with the
     heraldry of the Haberdashers. He is correct about the lion,
     but he has apparently confused the white goats that serve as
     supporters to the guild's arms with a unicorn. (See John
     Bromley, The Armorial Bearings of the Guilds of London
     (London: Warne, 1960), pp. 136-37).

255 Serve and obay] the motto of the Haberdashers.

257 a Magozin] a storehouse.

263 insidiate] to lie in wait for, to plot against (OED).

290 Negotior] to carry on business.

291 Miserior] to pity.

292 Largior] to give abundantly.

294 Patior: Precor] Patior: to suffer, undergo, experience;
     precor; to beg, entreat, pray.

298f Saint Katherin] included because Catherine of Alexandria
      (4th century) is the patron saint of the Haberdashers. In
      1448 the group was incorporated under the name of the
      "Fraternity of St. Katherine the Virgin of the Haberdasshers
      in the City of London" (Bromley, Armorial Bearings, p. 137).

Catherine had been represented in John Squire's 1620 mayoral
pageant, Triumphs of Peace.

304 concatinated] chained or linked together--OED cites this
     pageant text.

325 Wheele] the wheel, associated with Catherine, finds
     representation in the 15th-century version of the heraldic
     arms of the guild.

351 to my profection] to my advancement or place. OED cites
     this pageant for use of this word.

383f I cannot heare forget . . .] a revealing passage about
     the pageant dramatist's negotiations with the guild. It
     also, of course, flatters the guild.

396 literature] acquaintance with "letters" or books; polite
     or humane learning (OED)--The only sense of the term before
     the 18th century.

397 Tam Mercurio quam Marte periti] as expert for Mercury as
     for Mars (i.e., as much for trade as for war).

424 Mr. Gerard Christmas] the first of several times that the
     services of the artificer Gerard and his two sons, John and
     Mathias, will be utilized by Heywood. Christmas' career as
     artificer in civic pageants began in 1618; and he worked for
     Middleton, Dekker, and Heywood in preparing Lord Mayors'
     Shows. See for fuller discussion, David M. Bergeron, "The
     Christmas Family: Artificers in English Civic Pageantry,"
     ELH, 35 (1968), 354-64.

426-7 I shall . . . Unicorne] Heywood echoes, for example,
     Ben Jonson who in the 1604 royal entry pageant for King
     James wrote about the emblematic technique: under such
     circumstances it is not necessary to write, "This is a Dog;
     or, This is a Hare" (Herford & Simpson, Ben Jonson, VII,
     91).

430-31 I conclude with Plautus in sticho: Nam curiosus est nemo
     qui non sit malevolus] from Plautus' play Stichus: "No
     one is inquisitive without wishing the worst."

Londini Artium & Scientiarum Scaturigo:

or,

Londons Fountaine of Arts and Sciences:

Exprest in sundry Triumphs, Pageants, and Showes, at

the Initiation of the Right Honorable Nicholas Raynton

into the Maioralty of the famous and farre renowned

City London.

All the Charge and Expence of the laborious Projects both

by Water and Land, being the sole undertaking of the Right

Worshipfull Company of the Haberdashers,

Written by Thomas Haywood.

Redeunt Spectacula.

Printed at London by Nicholas Okes, 1632.

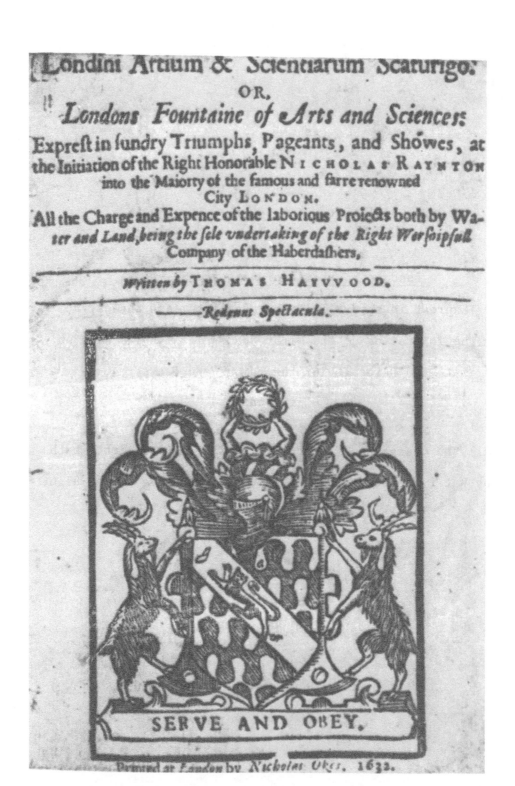

Title page of *Londini Artium & Scientiarum Scaturigo* (1632).
Reproduced by permission of the Huntington Library, San Marino,
California.

                    To the Right Honorable
                    Nicholas Raynton, Lord
             Maior of this renowned Metropolis
                         London.

Right Honourable,
Concerning the Dignity of your place, and Magnificence of your
Inauguration: The first equaling, the latter precelling all the
famous Magistracies in Christendome, I shall not much stand to
dispute, as being a Maxim already granted: yet one thing I cannot
omit, as most worthy remarke; namely, how many of like Judicature   10
have borne the Sword in this famous and florishing Citty, who
breathed their first ayre in the County of Lincolne; from whence you
derive your selfe, as Sir John Stockton Mercer, borne at Bratost,
Lord Maior 1470. Sir Nicholas Aldwin Mercer, borne at Spalding, Lord
Maior 1499. Sir William Rennington Fishmonger, at Bosten, Lord Maior
1500. Sir William Forman Haberdasher, at Gainsborow, Lord Maior
1538. Sir Henry Hobberthrone Merchant-Tayler, at Wadingworth, Lord
Maior 1546. Sir Henry Amcoats Fishmonger, at Astrop, Lord Maior
1548. Sir John Langley Goldsmith, at Althrop, Lord Maior 1576. Sir
John Allot Fishmonger, at Limbergh, Lord Maior 1590. Sir George
Bowles Grocer, at Gosperton, Lord Maior 1617. and now in present   20
your Honored selfe Nicholas Raynton borne at Heighington, Lord Maior
1632, not so many having attained to the same Dignity bred in any one
County, the City of London excepted. Worthy observation it is also,
that at one time in the raigne of Queene Elizabeth, most of the Prime
Officers of State, were Country-men of the same County: As the
Archbishop of Canterbury, Whitguift: the Lord High Treasurer of
England, Lord Burleigh Cecill, the Lord Keeper of the Great Seale,
Sir John Puckering, Viz-Chamberlaine and Chancellor of the Dutchy,
Sir Thomas Hennidge one of her Majesties Privy Councell: The Lord   30
Chiefe Justice, Judge Wraye, &c. Moreover it may be justly spoken of
you to your great Reputation and Honour, that since the yeere 1209,
from Henry Fitzalwin the first Lord Maior of this Honourable City,
and Peter Duke, and Thomas Neele the first Sheriffes of the same,
never had any Magistrate a more generall, free, and affectionate
Election even to this present Yeere 1632. Now Time and your owne
Demerit Right Honourable, have raysed you to this Eminence and
Dignity, the universall eye and expectation of all men is upon you,
who well know, that a wise Magistrate preferres Consideration before
Conclusion: And (according to the saying of King Agesilaus)   40
Magistrates who governe by just Lawes, must strengthen them by good
example: judge by Providence, Wisedome and Justice, and defend by
Power, Care and Vigilance; and thus I humbly take my leave of your
Lordship with this Sentence. Non sat est te tuum officium fecisse,
si non id fama approbat.

                    Your Lordship Countrey-
                    man and Servant,

                    Thomas Heywood.

To the Right
Worshipfull Hugh Perry, and Henry
Andrewes; the two Sheriffes of the
Honourable City London, last
Elected.

50

Right Worshipfull, and every way worthy; Your Armes display'd in the
Front of this Show, approve your Gentry, and your Trafficke and
Commerce, (being free Merchant-adventurers) testifie to the World
your Noble Profession; as Trading in the East-Indies, Turkey, Italy,
Spayne, and France, &c. to the Honour of our Nation abroad, and
singular Profits redounding to the Realme at home. Your more private
Imployments heretofore, aswell in furthering Arts, as incouraging
Armes, adding no common Luster to these Offices, unto which Time and
your owne Demerits have at this present called you. Then as that
Publicke weale is most blest and flourishing where the Governours are
aswell beloved in their Persons, as feared in their Places: So
likewise it belongeth to all such as are in Authority, to steare
themselves by the rule of Socrates, that is, To heare courteously,
answere discreetly, consider seriously, and sentence unpartially.
But I presume not to advise, where I rather desire to be instructed;
shutting up my present Service with that of Seneca, Id facere laus
est quod decet, non quod licet.

60

70

Your Worships to bee
commanded.

Thomas Heywood.

Londons Scaturigo.

The Title of the Show is <u>Scaturigo</u>, <u>i</u>. the Fountaine and Well-
spring of all the Liberall Arts, and Sciences, or Mysteries
whatsoever; which as they have beene long since planted, and
incouraged: so they are at this time the more liberally watered, and
therefore more plenteously inriched by their blessed Mother and
bountifull Nurse, the most illustrious Citty <u>London</u>: For the first,
namely, the Arts and Studies of the Braine; How many Grammer Schooles
have beene by her and her indulgent Children erected (through all, or
most of all) the Shieres and Counties of <u>England</u>, to the propagation
and advancement of Learning, to the furnishing of the Accademies with
Students, and from them, the foure flourishing Kingdomes (now under
the Sword and Scepter of his most Sacred Majesty) with profound
Theologists, expert Phisitians, learned Philosophers, skilfull
Mathematitians, &c. If any man desire to bee further instructed, in
the number of their Free-schooles, Hospitals, Almes-houses, Lectures,
Exercises (scarce to be numbred) with the names of the founders, and
the Annuall revenewes still continued, and dayly inlarged for their
perpetuall maintenance, I referre them unto our English Annalls,
where they may be plenteously satisfied; neither can these few Sheets
of Paper containe them, much rather require a Volumne.

So much for the Studies of the Braine.

Now for all other Sciences, Mysteries, Trades, and Manufactures,
(including aswell Merchants as Mechannicks) What City in <u>Europe</u>
yeeldeth more plenty? more variety? In so much that by reason of
Bartering, Bargening, Trade and Commerce, (besides the Busse or
Exchange, dayly throngd with Merchants of all Countries.) The
populous Streets rather appeare an open Mart, then an ordinary
Market; shee not favouring and fostering her owne Natives onely, but
Strangers, and of all forraigne Nations whatsoever. Here they sucke
the Milke of her brests, here they are fed, here cherished by this
excellent City, and therefore neither impertinently, nor unproperly
may shee be stiled: <u>Artium & Scientiarum inundans Scaturigo</u>.

The Show by Water.

It representeth <u>Arion</u> with his Harpe in his hand, riding upon the
backe of a Dolphin, behinde him for ornament old <u>Oceanus</u> and
<u>Amphetrite</u>, mounted upon two Sea-horses, holding each of them a
Staffe and a Banner, wherein are displayde the Armes of the two
Sherives now in place. Of him it is thus commented.

38

Arion was borne in Methimnus, whom Pyranthus, (or as Gellius and
Herodatus please to name him) Periander, for his excellent skill upon
the Harpe, greatly delighted in: Dycaearchus describeth him for a
noble Dithirambick Poet. He having got great store of Treasure, was
desirous to crosse from Corinth into Sicilia and Italy, to whom
Apollo appeares (the night before his imbarking) in a Dreame, and
willed him to attire himselfe in his Robe and Lawrell, and to be
ready in any danger to sing unto his Harpe, and not to feare any
thing. The next day (being farre from shoare) the Marriners having
notice what Treasure hee had aboord, conspired amongst themselves to
cast him into the Sea, which hee perceiving, begged of them so much
respite, that habited as hee was, hee might sing one funerall
farewell to his Harpe, which granted, so sweete was his Harmony, that
the Dolphins came sporting about the shippe, as much delighted with
his Musicke: amongst whom hee cast himselfe, and they supported him,
and bore him backe unto Corinth; where having told this wonderment,
the King graciously entertayned him; soone after the same Barke being
by a tempest droven into the same Harbour, notice thereof beeing
given unto the King, hee strictly questioned them concerning Arion;
they affirm'd him to bee dead at Sea, to which when they had sworne,
hee caused Arion suddenly to appeare before them, who confounded with
shame, were commanded to death: Appollo after translated Arion for
his Musicke, and the Dolphin for his Pitty amongst the Starres.

Lib. de Di-
onis. Certa-
minib.

120

130

Arions Speech directed to the River Thames.

    Faire Thamesis, upon whose silver brest
Arion with his Dolphin now doth rest.
How I admire thy Glory, State, and Pride,
Upon this Solemne day thus beautified?
Ganges renowned in all forraigne Lands,
Nor Tagus boasting of her golden Sands
Can paralell thy Riches; Not Caister
Famous for Swannes, nor Po her cleere stream'd Sister:
Winding Meander, nor yet Simois Flood,
Which Fame saith, at the Trojan Seige ran blood.
Swift Rubicon whose memory shall last,
Because it, Caesar with his Army past.
Choaspes, that almost guirts Persia round:
Nor Issa, by Darius death renown'd.
The Amazonian Thermedon, the Nyle
That breeds in it the weeping Crocadile.
The Euphrates, the Volga, and the Ryne,
Nay Jordan too, that waters Palestine:
What Paris Seine, or Romes swift Tyber bee,
The one a Brooke, the other a Ditch to thee:
And my Crownd Dolphin doth proclaime thee thus,
Th' art the choyse Darling of Oceanus.

The first
speech by
Water.
140

150

And if thou hast a <u>Genius</u>, (as 'tis guest   160
All Rivers have) know wherein th'art most blest.
Not that thy Bankes are so defenc't and stable,
Nor within Land th'art so far navigable,
Not for thy Flux and Refluxe, (Ebbs and Tydes)
Or the rich Meddowes bordering round thy sides.
Not that being pleas'd, th'art smooth, being angry, curl'd,
Nor thy rare Bridge not equald through the World.
Not for those goodly Buildings reard so hye,
To make thee live to perpetuity.
Not for thy spacious Limits and Extents,   170
(And yet all those unrivald Ornaments).

But if I truely shall to thee commend,
That blisse wherein thou others dost transcend,
Behold this Day the Honour and the State
Of this thy Great and God like Magistrate.
Not waited on by Boats made of the Trunks
Of Canes, or hollowed Trees, or petty Junks,
Or wanton Gondelaes: but Barges, strong,
And richly deckt, who as they plowe along
Thy brest, with their smooth keeles to make their way,
See how the Wind doth with their streamers play,   180
How beautiful thy Waves, how throngd thy shoares,
And what a Musick's when they strike their Oares.
To see them with Grave Magistrates so Man'd,
Powerfull by Sea, and potent too by Land.
So many Sciences, and Misteries
Distinguisht into severall Companies,
In sundry bottomes: and each Art and Trade
Knowne by the Flags and Pendants here displaid.
And <u>London</u> which <u>Metropolis</u> we call,
The <u>Fount</u> and <u>Scaturigo</u> of them all.   190

Grave <u>Praetor</u>, now this Day to be invested
The Head of al these, passe on unmolested,
In your great Inauguration proceede,
Which to your lasting Honour is decreed.
In your returne backe you shall understand,
Those Triumphs that attend on you by Land.

<u>Perseus</u>, <u>Andromeda</u> with the Sea-monster are onely shewed upon the
Water, but their expression I referre to their place by Land.

Of which the first presentment is in <u>Pauls</u> Churchyard: Namely,   <u>The first</u>
St. <u>Katherine</u>, Patronesse of this Worshipfull Company, upon a Lyon,   <u>Show by</u>
bordered about with the Sea-waves (the Armes of the Haberdashers).   <u>Land</u>.
Shee is Crowned as being a Queene, bearing a Wheele in her hand, full
of sharpe cutting Irons, the Embleame of her Martyrdome: Her
attendants to beautifie the plat-forme, are foure Virgins, <u>Humility</u>

40

the first: Of which Vertue <u>Seneca</u> thus speaketh, <u>Laus vera humili</u>
<u>sepe contingit viro</u>. The second <u>Truth</u>, which scaleth the Heavens,
illustrateth the Earth, maintaineth Justice, governeth Cities, kils
Hatred, cherisheth Love, and discovereth Treasons: The third <u>Zeale</u>,
of which it is thus sayd; <u>Office is strengthned by Zeale, and Zeale</u>
<u>maketh authority invincible</u>, The fourth, <u>Constancy</u>: according with
that of <u>Lucan</u>, <u>Intrepidus quicunque datis mihi Numina mortem Accipiam</u>
----- All which are necessary in a Magistrate, as needfull in a
Martyr: Of the Etymologie of her Name, her Royal Birth, her
Breeding, her Life and Death, in the last yeeres Discourse I gave a
large Charactar, and therefore proceede to her Speech, which is as
followeth.

St. <u>Katherines</u> Speech.

Doth any wonder, why St. <u>Katherine</u>, shee
The Patronesse of this faire Companie
Is mounted on a Lyon? Let such know,
That (being a Queene) this kingly beast doth owe
Mee duty by instinct: Besides I come
Both with Virginity and Martyrdome,
Sainted moreover, and (of these) the least
Able to tame, the most insulting Beast.
But this is hee the billowes doth devide,
And therefore justly on his backe I ride:
All these belonging to this Worthy Trade,
The <u>Lyon</u>, <u>Sea-waves</u>, and the <u>Princely Mayde</u>.

That for the Armes: note next what I display
In this my Banner here, <u>Serve and obey</u>:
Rare Morall in this Motto, (if well scand)
For Kings are Gods, Viz-gerents, and command
By Sword and Scepter: and by their good Grace
Can preferre others both to power and place.

As you this Day behold this Scarlet worne,
And Sword of Justice thus in publike borne;
The Cap of Maintenance, Coller of Esses,
(Which Travellers in all their large progresses
Can in no City parallell, that's scite
In th' earths devision, knowne quadrupertite):
So, whosoever shall himselfe oppose
Against this Magistrate, (as one of those
The King deputes as Chiefe) himselfe hee brings
To bee a rebell to the King of Kings:
Far be it an arch-traytor in that kind
'Mongst all these goodly Companies, (combind
In mutuall love and league) should dare to appeare

Senec. in
Thiest.

210
Lib. 5. de
bell. Civil.

St. Kathe-
rins speech.

230

240

In the faire Progresse of this <u>Praetors</u> yeare.

Behold, and view who my attendants bee,   250
<u>Constancy</u>, <u>Zeale</u>, <u>Truth</u>, and <u>Humility</u>.
Be constant then unto this Grave Lord <u>Maior</u>,
And the two <u>Shrieves</u> that his assistants are;
Chose by the <u>publicke</u> Voyce and Senats Doome,
As <u>Censors</u>, and the <u>Tribunes</u> were in <u>Rome</u>;
Doe it in Zeale, in Truth, and all submission,
That there be found no crosse interposition
Betwixt <u>Power</u> and <u>Obedience</u>, so shall all
Arts, Mysteries, and Trades Mechannicall,
Thrive, prosper, and increase so long as they   260
Honour the King, the Magistrate obey.

The second show by Land.

This discovereth <u>Andromeda</u> the Daughter of King <u>Cepheus</u>, and
<u>Cassiopeia</u>, tide to a <u>Rocke</u>, and ready to bee devoured by a Sea-
monster: But rescued by <u>Perseus</u> the Sonne of <u>Jupiter</u> and <u>Danae</u>, who
is mounted upon a <u>Pegasus</u>, or Winged-horse, who is sayd to bee bred
from <u>Neptune</u> and <u>Medusa</u>, and in <u>Hellicon</u> a Mountaine in <u>Boetia</u>,
striking a Stone with his hoofe, opend that Fountaine called (from
him) <u>Hyppocrene</u>, much celebrated by the <u>Muses</u>. <u>Perseus</u> in one hand
hath an <u>Harpe</u> or crooked Sword, and upon his left arme a <u>Shield</u> with   270
a <u>Gorgons</u> head figured therein: In <u>Perseus</u> are comprehended all the
prime Vertues acquired in a Noble Magistrate: In <u>Andromeda</u> <u>Chastity</u>
and <u>Innocence</u>: I cannot heere insist upon the Hystory, but rather
referre the Reader to <u>Ovid</u>, who hath most elegantly expressed it; but   <u>Lib</u>. Meta-
come to the Speech delivered by <u>Perseus</u>.   <u>mor</u>.

Perseus his Speech.

I <u>Perseus</u>, <u>Joves</u> sonne, borne of Heavenly Seede,
Mounted upon a swift <u>Pegasian</u> Steede,
Who with his hoofe strooke up the <u>Muses</u> Well,
Whence <u>Euthusiasma's</u> and hie Ruptures swell.   280
As through the ayery tract I forc't my way,
Spyde here the Lovely Maide <u>Andromeda</u>,
Cheynd to a Rocke, on whom (so Fate hath lowerd)
Ready by a Sea-whale to be devourd.

Know there is figured in this <u>Princely</u> <u>Maide</u>,
<u>Chastity</u>, and <u>Innocence</u>, which Divine ayde
Is ready to assist still from above,

42

By one or other of the Sonnes of <u>Jove</u>.
Of which denomination, none, more Grace
Can claime than you, who are in power and place,   290
And hold this Day in chiefe; then <u>Perseus</u> like,
Keepe that your <u>Sword</u> still drawne, ready to strike;
Making such Monsters of your Justice tast,
Who insidiate the Innocuous and the Chaste.

 Observe (<u>Graue</u> <u>Sir</u>) the <u>Armes</u> and <u>Shield</u> I beare,
Such as yourselfe, and others ought to weare,
Both for Defence and Offence: and in me
Embleam'd, all those prime Vertues that should be
In Persons of your Power, my <u>Sword</u> resembles
<u>Unpartiall</u> <u>Justice</u>, at which guilt still trembles;   300
My Winged-horse, Celerity and Speed:
In doing it, that no illegal deed
May passe unscourged, and there be tooke no rest,
Until reliefe be given to the opprest.

 This <u>Shield</u> that beares the Gorgons head imblaz'd,
Upon whose Snaky locks who ever gaz'd,
Were turn'd to statues of cold senselesse stone,
Is that (<u>Grave</u> <u>Magistrate</u>) you now put on.
Whilst on your Arme you weare this constant <u>Targe</u>,
Bearing yourselfe uprightly in your Charge.   310
All such as shal in Malice or in Pride
Your Purple State detract from, or deride,
Discover this before them, it hath power
To freeze them into Marble the same houre.
Strive you to imitate what I have done,
Since you this day, are <u>Perseus</u> and <u>Joves</u> sonne.

<u>The</u> <u>third</u> <u>show</u> <u>by</u> <u>Land</u>.

 This is more Mimicall then Materiall, and inserted for the
Vulgar, who rather love to feast their eyes, then to banquet their
eares: and therefore though it bee allowed place amongst the rest:
(as in all Professions wee see Dunces amongst Doctors, Simple amongst
Subtle, and Fooles intermixt with Wisemen to fill up number) as
doubting whether it can wel appollogy for itselfe or no, at this time
I affoord it no tongue.

The fourth show by Land.

The Right Honourable the Lord Maior in present, though free of
this Worshipfull Company of the Haberdashers, (at whose sole charge,
the High Solemnity of this Day is celebrated) yet was by Profession a
Mercer, and his chiefe Trading was in Florence for Sattins,   330
Taffaties, and Sarsnets; in Luca for Taffaties and Sarsnets, in Gene
for Gene Velvets, Damasks, &c. In Bolognia for Satins, Cypresse, and
Sarsnets. As also in Pysa, now because the materialls of which these
Stuffes are made, are brought from the farthest remote Countries upon
the backs of Cammels, Mules, Dromidaries and Elephants: I made
choice of this Beast, especially, of whose incomparable strength and
most pregnant understanding, if any desire to be fully satisfied, I
must referre them to Pliny, Gesner, but more essentially to Don
Sebastian de Corbarrvias Orozco En el Tesoro de la Lengua Castellana,
(from whom Minshaw borrowed his Etymologicall Spanish Dictionary)
upon the word Elephante, where are divers Stories of them, which but   340
for the Gravity of the Author, might almost appeare incredible. The
Elephant is guided by an Indian, upon his backe is a faire Castle
furnisht with change and variety of objects, &c. the Speech delivered
by the Indian as followeth.

The Indians Speech.

No beast of all the Wildernesse can vant
Like Strength or Wisedome with the Elephant.
And therefore, (if considered wel) none may
Better become the Triumphs of this Day.
What Hieroglificke can a man invent,   350
Embleame or Symbole, for a Government
In this high nature, apter or more fit
Devis'd before, or to be thought of yet.

He beares a Castle (as this day wee see),
But of what strength and puissance must you bee
Supporting this great Citty? who must lay
Your shoulders to a burden; such as may
Make Atlas shrinke beneath it; Temples, Towers,
Rialtoes, spacious Mansions, Suburbe bowers.
A weight to make th' Hesperian Giant droope   360
And Hercules, (who bore up Heaven) to stoope.

Next, of what Understanding, Apprehension,
What Judgement, Knowledge, Wisedome and Retention?
Of what Fore-sight? what Body and what Braine?
What an Antomedan to guide the raine
Of Steedes unmannag'd? what a Palinure

Antomed.
Hectors
Charioter.
Palinur: Pi-
lot to AEneas

44

To steare this Helme? and such a Barke assure
In a Sea troubled, where can be no trust
In an unconstant Surge or angry Gust?

    Yet such an <u>Elephant</u> we hope to finde   370
Of you, both in th' ability of Minde
And strength of Arme, by that incouragement
The former passage of your life hath lent:
Showed in your <u>Judgement</u> and <u>Experience</u>,
Your <u>Gravity</u>, and unchang'd <u>Temperance</u>;
All generall Vertues that become such State,
Behovefull in so Great a Magistrate:
So after Times unto you Fame shall story
How you have borne up in her pristine Glory
This flourishing City, not once shrinking under   380
So great a burden, (to successive wonder)
Since no skild Pilot better could command
By Sea, or expert Charioter by Land.

The <u>fift</u> <u>show</u> <u>by</u> <u>Land</u>.

    Is the <u>Scaturigo</u> or Fountaine of Vertue, from which all Arts and
Sciences are watered: I neede not to spend Time in the description
thereof, it being able sufficiently to expresse it selfe, the nature
thereof being in the Poeme layd open even unto the meanest capacity.
There are twelve sundry persons to beautifie the Modell, suiting with
the number of the twelve Companies, as the Saints that patronize   390
them; and every of them a Shield on their arme, bearing their several
Scutchions properly belonging to the Halls. The Speech from the
Fountaine is thus delivered.

The <u>Speech</u> <u>upon</u> <u>the</u> <u>Fountaine</u>.

    Twelve houres twice told, distinguish night and Day,
Twelve <u>Caesars</u> of the <u>Julian</u> Line did sway
<u>Romes</u> Empire, and in every case of striffe
Where Action's tryde or if concerning life,
Twelve makes the Jury full: the <u>Zodaiacke</u> Lines
Are likewise fild by twelve <u>Celestiall</u> Signes,   400
Amongst which one in your Emblazons borne
Is numbred by the name of <u>Capricorne</u>.
Twelve <u>Sibills</u> we account, and they fore-told
Things hapned since, although they spake of old
By twelve: the blest Word in the Church instated
Was at the first divuldg'd and propagated.

Twelve Companies you are in Chiefe, 12. heere
Present that number with those Armes they beare.
And hence the Inundant Scaturigo growes,
Which through our Kingdomes large Dominions flowes,   410
By founded Schooles, by Colledges, by Trade,
By Trafficke, by Commerce, by Project, layd.
For thrifty Bargaine and all competent Gayne,
Aswell arising from the Hand as Brayne.
London the Mother and the Fountaine stil'd.
And you of all her Sonnes now eldest Child;
(Heire to her good Workes) incourage still
Those pious Acts, and by Example fill
Voide places with the like, and in this State
You beare, as being now chiefe Magistrate: 420
So order this your numerous Charge, that they
May God, the King, Your selfe Serve and Obey.

A word or two concerning the supporters of the Armes of this   Of the Sup-
Worshipfull Company. Parmenisius a Greek Author thus relates, King   porters of
Melliseus who ruled in Creete, had two Daughters, to whom Jupiter in the Armes of
his Infancy was sent to be nursed, to preserve him from the fury of the Company.
his Father Saturne: but they being at that time dry-brested, caused
him to sucke of a Goate called Amalthaea, by whose Milke hee was
nourished, till the time that hee came to be weyned, (this Goate
usually brought forth two twins). Jupiter after in requitall of so   430
great a benefit received by her, translated her amongst the Starres.
This Goate is that Capricornus one of the 12. Celestiall Signes. The
two Kidds (her twins) placed in the Heavens also, were first observed
by the great Astrologer Cleostrates Tenedius. The last Speech at
Night is delivered by Arion, which is a short commemoration of the
former passages of the Dayes Triumph in these wordes following.

Now hath the Sun put off his golden beames,
Watring his hot Steeds in cold Ister streames,
And tyr'd with his dayes travell, in the West
Tooke up his Inne: But ere you goe to rest,   440
Remember what Arion still proclaimes
In the due honour of the noble Thames.
Next, how your Queene-like Saint directs the way
For you to rule, for others to obey
Then to be cal'd Joves Sonne you have the Grace,
And that in Perseus figured is your Place.
That in this able Elephant's implyde
Your strength to beare, your Judgement to decyde.
Last, that you are the Spring and Fountaine made
To water every Science, Art, and Trade;   450
Observing those, your Honour shall shine bright,
And so a happy and most blest good-night.

I come last to the Artist, the Moddellor and Composer of these severall Peeces, Maister Gerard Christmas, of whom (si paruis componere, magna licet) as Augustus Caesar, speaking of Rome, boasted, that hee found it of Bricke, but hee left it built of Marble: So he who found these Pageants and showes of Wicker and Paper, rather appearing monstrous and prodigious Births, then any Beast (presented in them) in the least kind imitating Nature: hath reduc't them to that sollidity and substance for the Materialls, that   460 they are so farre from one dayes washing to deface them, that the weathering of many Winters can not impeach them: and for their excellent Figures and well-proportioned lineaments, (by none preceding him) that could be sayd to bee paralleld: In regard therefore there bee so many strangers of all Countries, and such as can judge of Workemanship, come to be spectators of these Annuall Triumphs, I could wish that the undertaking thereof might be hereafter conferd (for the Honour of the Citty) upon men like able and sufficient. For his owne particular I conclude: Hunc aliquis vix imitando superare potest.

FINIS.   470

Textual Notes

Londini Artium & Scientiarum Scaturigo, Heywood's second mayoral pageant (Greg, Bibliography, no. 466; STC 13347) exists in two copies, one in the Huntington Library and the other in the library of Worcester College, Oxford. They represent two different issues of the same edition with the Worcester copy apparently being the earlier and less correct version. A. M. Clark edited this pageant text in "Two Pageants by Thomas Heywood; 1632, 1633," in Theatre Miscellany: Six Pieces connected with the Seventeenth-Century Stage (Oxford: Luttrell Society Publications no. 14, 1953), pp. 1-47. Clark offers essentially a diplomatic reprint of the text; he follows the Huntington copy.

On pp. 46-47 of the Clark edition, John Crow analyzes the relationship between the two issues, concluding that the Huntington copy represents the corrected version and that these corrections have Heywood's authority. My own investigation and conclusions correspond to Crow's, though I admit that the evidence is not always clear. The title page, sig. A1, remains unchanged, and sig. A2 is blank in both copies. The inner forme of Sheet A was reset with numerous spelling and punctuation changes. In the Collation below, I note the significant changes without recording punctuation changes; I offer the evidence as a means of defining the relationship between the two texts. Crow says that A2 was entirely reset without "verbal change"; but, as the notes below indicate, that assertion is not accurate. Sig. A2 of the original text is found on lines 1-25 of this edition. Certainly, for example, the change in l. 7 from "latter" to "later" must be considered a verbal change; in l. 9 "a Maxim" becomes "Maxims" in the Worcester copy. On sig. A2^v, beginning with line 31 of this edition, several lines are taken from sig. A3 of the Worcester copy and correctly placed here. Obviously A3 and A3^v were reset. The type of A4 was used in both texts with two (not one as Crow says) small press-corrections made in the standing type: see lines 75 and 82. Press variants occur on sig. B1 (margin) and on C1^v; these are recorded below. Again, one must alter Crow's statement that "otherwise the pages are identical in the two copies." I use the Huntington copy for the copy-text for this edition.

Collation

(title page) Maioralty] Maiorty Q

  6 Magnificence] Hunt; Magnifiecence Wor

  7 latter] Hunt; later Wor

  9 a Maxim] Hunt; Maxims Wor

48

16   Rennington] Hunt; Renningeton Wor

16   Bosten] Hunt; Boston Wor

18   Merchant-Tayler] Hunt; Marchant Taylor Wor

31-36 Moreover . . . 1632] Hunt; omitted in Wor

67   answere] Hunt; answer Wor

68   instructed] Hunt; instracted Wor

71   bee] Hunt; be Wor

75   Scaturigo, i.] Hunt; Scaturigo. i. Wor

82   (through] Hunt; ,through Wor

91   inlarged] inlarged? Q

91   their] heir Q

92   maintenance,] maintenance? Q

155 Seine] Some Q

207 illustrateth] illustateth Q

257 there] their Q

278 swift] swist Q (Clark emends but without nothing his change)

300 trembles;] Hunt; trembles Wor

301 -horse,] Hunt; -horse; Wor

318 (margin) by Land] Hunt; by water Wor

338 Corbarrvias Orozco] Corbarruias Orozeo Clark

378 you] your Q

383 Charioter] Charicter Q

397 striffe] Hunt; strife Wor

414 Aswell] Asswell Q

Commentary Notes

This pageant, honoring Sir Nicholas Raynton, Haberdasher, was Heywood's second for this particular guild. Again, one finds in the guild records payments of £2 for printing 300 copies of the text, and a payment of £190 to Gerard Christmas "for Pageants" (Collections, p. 122). No information comes from the records regarding Heywood's negotiations with the guild nor his payment. Presumably, Christmas paid Heywood out of his sum.

Vicenzo Gussoni, Venetian Ambassador in London, reports: "Two days ago they celebrated the usual early but stately ceremony of the Mayor, the magistrate of London. It is usual to invite the ambassadors, but France could not go, being in mourning for his mother, recently deceased, and so it fell to the minister of your Serenity to take the first place at the head of that rich and sumptuous procession, followed by the two Dutch ministers, by the great lords of the realm and by other lords of the royal Council" (Calendar of State Papers Venetian, XXIII, 28). As in the court masque, so in the civic pageant: there was constant concern among the ambassadorial corps about precedence.

12   Lincolne] Heywood was himself born in Lincolnshire.

13-22   John Stockton . . . Nicholas Raynton] John Stockton, Lord Mayor 1471, son to Richard Stockton, one of the twelve aldermen who were knighted for opposing the bastard Falconbridge. Nicholas Aldwin, son to Richard Alwin [Alwyn], gave twelve pence a piece to 3000 poor people in London, and the like to the poor of Spalding. William Rennington, son to Roger Remington of Boston. William Forman, sheriff 1533, Alderman for Cripplegate, MP for London 1545, died 1547. Henry Hobberthorne, son to Christopher Hobblethorne (Hubbarthorne). Henry Amcoats, son to William Amcotes, died 1554. John Langley, son of Robert Langely. John Allot, son of Richard Allot; the 1590 Lord Mayor's Show by Thomas Nelson was prepared in Allot's honor. George Bowles, born 1538, Warden of the Grocers' 1599, Master of the company 1606; Alderman of Dowgate 1607 and of Walbrook 1616 until his death in 1621; Sheriff 1608; as mayor in 1617 he was honored by a Lord Mayor's Show written by Thomas Middleton, died 1621. Nicholas Raynton, sheriff 1621, president of St. Bartholomew's Hospital; died 1646.

27   Archbishop . . . Whitguift] John Whitgift (?1530-1604); eldest son of Henry Whitgift of Lincolnshire; took holy orders in 1560; elected Dean of Lincoln in 1571; Bishop of Worcester 1577; Archbishop in 1583.

28   Burleigh Cecill] William Cecil (1520-1598), knighted 1551; represented Lincolnshire in Parliament; appointed

Chief Secretary of State by Queen Elizabeth; became Lord High Treasurer in 1572.

29 John Puckering] (1544-1596), Lord Keeper of the Great Seal, made Lord Keeper in April 1592; MP, Speaker of the House.

30 Thomas Hennidge] Heneage; died 1595; vice-chamberlain of Elizabeth's household; auditor of the duchy of Lancaster; MP for Lincolnshire in parliaments 1571 and 1572 and for Essex from 1585 until his death.

31 Judge Wraye] Christopher Wray (1524-1592), represented Lincolnshire in Parliament for several years; Speaker of the House 1571; appointed justice 1572; and Chief Justice of the Queen's Bench 1574.

33-34 Fitzalwin . . . Neele] all three were mentioned by Heywood in the 1631 pageant.

37 Demerit] merit or desert (see l. 62 below).

40-42 according to the saying of King Agesilaus . . . good example] such an idea is found in the story of Agesilaus in North's translation of Plutarch; or in Xenophon, Scripta Minora, vii. 2: "For who would be minded to disobey [the laws] when he saw the king obeying?"

44-45 Non sat est te tuum officium fecisse, si non id fama approbat] "It is not enough for you to have done your duty if fame does not approve of it."

50-51 Hugh Perry, and Henry Andrewes] Perry, Mercer, sheriff 1632, Alderman of Queenhithe, died 1635. Andrewes, Haberdasher, Master of the company 1633-4; Alderman Farringdon Within; sheriff 1532, died August 1638.

66-67 the rule of Socrates, that is, To heare . . . sentence unpartially] something similar to this can be found in Plato's Apology. As with much of this kind of material Heywood has borrowed it probably from some Latin author writing about the Greeks.

69-70 Seneca, Id facere . . . licet] "It is praiseworthy to do what is proper, not what is possible." Again, not to be found in Seneca's works.

75 i.] meaning i.e.--acceptable abbreviation.

92 our English Annalls] possibly Stow's Annals or Camden's Annales.

99-100 Busse or Exchange] refers to the New Exchange or "Britain's Burse" opened in the Strand in 1609. Busse = obsolete form of burse.

113-115 Arion] Aulus Gellius in his Attic Nights repeats the story, largely based on Herodotus, in Book XVI, 19. Arion is several times represented in pageants, as in the Kenilworth entertainment of 1575. In Book I of Herodotus the author discusses the story of Arion, saying "he was the first man, as far as we know, to compose and name the dithyramb."

115 Dycaearchus] Dichaearchus, a Greek from Messana, a pupil of Aristotle and contemporary of Theophrastus. Only fragments of his work survive, one of which concerns competitions in music and poetry. Cicero refers to him in De Officiis, Book II, 5, 16, and also in some of his letters.

115 (margin) Lib. de Dionis. Certaminib.] probably a reference to a book about the muses' contests. The Oxford Classical Dictionary reports that such a book was an important source for later scholars but survives only in fragments, most if not all of them quotations by later scholars.

141f Ganges . . . Issa] a series of rivers. Ganges, India; Tagus, Lisbon; Caister, Kuenk Menderes River in West Turkey; Po, Chinese rivers; Meander, winding river in Phrygia; Simois, small river of Troas, now in Turkey; Choaspes, or Karkheh River in Iran; Issa, a Russian river.

200 St. Katherine] see the 1631 pageant where she is also represented. Heywood refers to this earlier pageant in l. 214.

205-6 Seneca thus speaketh, Laus vera humili sepe contingit viro] in Seneca's Thyestes, "True praise even to the lowly often comes."

211 Lucan, Intrepidus quicunque datis mihi Numina mortem Accipiam] in Book 5, line 658 of the Civil Wars, "I shall not slink from meeting whatever end Heaven appoints for me."

231 Serve and obey] motto of the Haberdashers.

263 Andromeda] cf. the treatment of the Perseus-Andromeda story in Heywood's Troia Britanica or Great Britaines Troy (London, 1609), canto VI.

274 referre the Reader to Ovid] Book V of the Metamorphoses.

318-324 This is . . . no tongue] Heywood is more conscious or
at least more overt than other pageant dramatists at
creating some scene that has no purpose other than display.
Perhaps Heywood is the only pageant writer to bother to
record such activity in his printed text.

330 Gene] acceptable English spelling for Genoa.

337-339 Don Sebastian . . . Spanish Dictionary] Don
Sebastian, whose name has several spellings, published his
Tesoro in Madrid in 1611. Minshaw is John Minsheu (fl.
1617) who in 1617 published The Guide into Tongues (STC
17944), which underwent many editions. He also expanded
Richard Percyvall's A Dictionarie in Spanish and English
(STC 19620).

337 I must referre them to Pliny, Gesner] Pliny's Natural
History, Book VIII on the subject of elephants. Conrad
Gesner, Historiae Animalium (1585).

346 vant] (vaunt), to boast or proclaim (OED).

424-425 Parmenisius a Greeke Author thus relates, King Melliseus
who ruled] one of two persons may be the Parmeniscus
alluded to by Heywood: a Parmeniscus of Metapontum,
probably 5th century B.C., ranked by Iamblichus as among the
celebrated Pythagorean philosophers; or a Parmeniscus, a
grammarian and commentator. The daughters of Melliseus were
Adrastea and Ida, to whom Rhea entrusted the infant Zeus to
be brought up.

434 Astrologer Cleostrates Tenedius] Cleostratus an
astronomer of Tenedos, probably lived 548-432 B.C. Pliny
says that he introduced the division of the Zodiac into
signs, beginning with Aries and Sagittarius.

454 Gerard Christmas] artificer, to whom Heyood referred in
the 1631 text (see note there).

454-55 si paruis componere, magna licet] this means, more or
less, "If one can compose small things, he can large ones,
too."

455 Augustus Caesar] the episode is reported in Suetonius,
The Twelve Caesars.

469 Hunc aliquis vix imitando superare potest] "One can
hardly surpass him by imitating."

Londini Emporia,

or

Londons Mercatura.

Exprest in sundry Triumphs, Pageants and
Showes, at the Inauguration of the Right Honorable
Ralph Freeman into the Maioralty of the
Famous and farre Renowned
Citty London.
All the Charge and Expence of the laborious Projects, both
by Water and Land, being the sole undertaking of the Right
Worshipfull Company of the Cloath-Workers,

Written by Thomas Heywood.

Redeunt Spectacula.

Printed at London by Nicholas Okes, 1633.

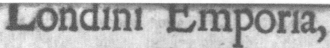

Londini Emporia,

OR

Londons Mercatura.

Expreſt in ſundry Triumphs, Pageants and
Showes, at the Inauguration of the Right Honorable
RALPH FREEMAN into the Maiorty of the
Famous and farre Renowned
Citty LONDON.

All the Charge and Expence of the laborious Proiects, both
by Water and Land, being the ſole vndertaking of the Right
Worſhipfull Company of the Cloath-Workers.

Written by THOMAS HEYVVOOD.

——— *Redeunt Spectacula.* ———

MY TRVST IS IN GOD ALONE.

Printed at *London* by *Nicholas Okes,* 1633.

Title page of *Londini Emporia* (1633). Reproduced by permission of the
Huntington Library, San Marino, California.

To the Right Honourable Ralph Freeman, Lord

Maior of this Renowned Me-

tropolis London.

Right Honourable,
    The Triumphs and Sollemnities of this Day, are dedicated and
devoted to this your happy Inauguration, which as Time warranteth, so
Custome confirmeth: And herein hath this City a Priority above any
Metropolis in Europe: For Rome it selfe when the Monarchy of the
world was under her sole Jurisdiction, never received her Praetor,
Consul, or Dictator with the like Pompe and Sollemnity: yet is it
derived unto you from Antiquity, and I wish it may continue to all
Posterity. And Sir, for your owne part I am not altogether
unacquainted with your Modesty, which would willingly have evaded
this honourable trouble, but now you finde that the Condition of
Honour is such, that it inquireth after him who regardeth it not,
courteth him that affecteth it not, and followeth him fastest who
most flyeth it, as knowing that it is not the Place which maketh the
Person, but the Person which maketh the Place truely Honourable,
which now hath invited you to your merit, howsoever against your
minde, according to that of the famous Historiographer Lyvi. Decad.
Lib. 4. Gratia & honos opportuniores interdum non cupientibus sunt.
Advising you withall to this your high Office and Calling, to observe
the necessary adjuncts thereto belonging, namely, Affability with
Authority, and with your Sword and Power, Commiseration and Pitty:
Neither can I wish you a better President to imitate then your
Predecessor, of whom I may say, Semper honos nomenque suum laudesque
manebunt. Not questioning but that wee may speake the like of your
selfe, and the two worthy Gentlemen the Sheriffes, your Assistants,
when Time shall summon you to resigne your places to these which
shall succeed you: And thus I humbly take my leave of your Lordship,
with this Sentence borrowed from Seneca, Bonum est laudari, sed
praestantius est esse laudabilem.

                    Your Lordships humbly devoted,

                      Thomas Heywood.

56

LONDONS EMPORIA,

or

MERCATURA.

    Mercatura, i. Merchandise, the Greekes call Emporia, and Emporos,
a Merchant, the Hebrewes Meker. From hence (it seems) the Poets call
Hermes (the Sonne of Jupiter and Maia) Mercury, making him the God of
Merchants and Merchandise. The mistery whereof hath in the ancient
times beene held glorious, and the professors thereof illustrious as
those, by whose Adventure and Industry unknowne Countries have beene
discovered, Friendship with forreigne Princes contracted, barbarous
Nations to humane gentlenesse and courtesie reduced, and all such
usefull commodities in forreigne Climats abounding, and in their owne
wanting, made conducible and frequent, nay, many of them have not
beene onely the Erectors of brave and goodly structures, but the
Founders of great and famous Cities (for so sayth Plutarch in Solon):
Merchandise it selfe, according to Aristotle consisteth of three
things, Navigation, Foeneration, and Negotiation, all which are
commendably approved, if considerately and conscionably used.

    Eight Offices of Piety are in a Merchant required. 1. Rectitudo
conscientiae, Uprightnesse of Conscience, which is most acceptable to
the Creator, (and therefore ought to be more prized by the Creature)
then any vaine-glorious Title: as stiled by our best Theologists,
the indulgent Mother of all Vertues whatsoever. 2. Simulationis &
dissimulationis seclusio, i. A seclusion or separation from all
dissembling or equivocation. 3. Fraudem devitare, i. To abandon
all fraud or deceite in bargaining, but in all Covenants and
Contracts to observe truth and irreprooveable fidelity. 4.
Justitiam exerceri, i. To exercise Justice: which excludeth the
practice of Injury, Extortion, and Oppression. 5. Superbiam
deponere, To lay by all pride, for (as divine Plato sayth) Hee who
knoweth himselfe best, esteemeth of himselfe the least: Wee reade
also in Socrates, that pride is a vice which of young men ought to be
carefully avoided, of old men utterly abjured, of all men suspected
and feared. 6. Beneficientia uti, i. Out of his abundance to bee
open-handed unto all, but especially unto the poore and indigent. 7.
Avaritiam froenare, i. To bridle the insatiate desire of getting,
for the avaritious man wanteth as well what he hath, as what he hath
not: who hath great travaile in gathering Wealth, more danger in
keeping it, much Law in defending it, most torment in departing from
it. 8. Sollicitudines resecare, i. To renounce all care and
trouble of minde, which may hinder Divine contemplation, but rather
to fixe his thoughts upon that Heavenly treasure which the Moath
corrupteth not, the Fire cannot waste, nor the Sea wracke: All these
things desireable being knowne to be eminent in your Lordship, was

40

Lib. Pol.

60

70

the maine inducement to intitle this present Show by this apt
Denomination, <u>Londini</u> <u>Emporia</u>:   Further of Merchants we reade <u>Horace</u>   80
thus,

<u>Impiger</u> extremos <u>currit</u> <u>Mercator</u> <u>ad</u> <u>Indos</u>,   <u>Horat</u>. <u>lib</u>. <u>I</u>.
<u>Per mare</u> <u>pauperiem</u> <u>fugiens</u>, <u>per saxa per</u> <u>ignes</u>.   <u>Epist</u>. <u>I</u>.
The <u>Merchant</u> <u>to</u> <u>the</u> farthest <u>Indies</u> <u>flies</u>,
<u>Through</u> seas, <u>rockes</u>, <u>fires</u>, <u>lest</u> <u>Want</u> should <u>him</u> <u>surprise</u>.

Concerning this Company of the Cloath-workers, none hath beene
more ancient, as claiming their place from the first institution, and
though in count the last of Twelve, yet everyway equall with the
first or any: the reasons are pregnant, and briefely these: The
Nobility of the Land are called <u>Pares</u>, (that is) Peeres. For their
parity and equality, as having prevalent voyces in the high Session,   90
or Court of Parliament. The two famous Universities are equall
Sisters: neyther can one claime priority above the other, yet
because they cannot be named at once, those of <u>Cambridge</u> say,
<u>Cambridge</u> and <u>Oxford</u>: Those of <u>Oxford</u> say <u>Oxford</u> and <u>Cambridge</u>,
which neither addeth nor detracteth from the other: In all numbers
there is a compulsive necessity of order, onely for method sake, not
that we can properly say, this Figure in it selfe is better then
that, being all of them onely helpers to make up an Account: since
that all the Lord Maiors of this honourable City (from which the
Twelve Companies soever they be Elected) beare one Sword, receive one   100
Power, and retaine like Authority: (There being no difference at all
in place, office, or in granting Priviledges or Immunities &c.) I
hold them all equall without difference, or if any shall claime
priority or precedence above the rest, let it bee conferr'd upon that
which breedeth the best Magistrates, and of this Company have beene
these after named, not of the least Eminence, as Sir <u>William</u> <u>Hart</u>,
Lord Maior <u>Anno</u> 1559. Sir <u>Rowland</u> <u>Hayward</u> <u>Anno</u> 1570, who was twice
Lord Maior at the least. Sir <u>James</u> <u>Howell</u> <u>Anno</u> 1574. Sir <u>Edward</u>
<u>Osborne</u> <u>Anno</u> 1583. <u>Thomas</u> <u>Skinner</u>, who dyed before hee was <u>Knighted</u>,
1596. Sir <u>John</u> <u>Spencer</u> <u>Anno</u> 1594. Sir <u>Michael</u> <u>Moseley</u> 1599. Sir   110
<u>John</u> <u>Watts</u> 1606. And now this present yeare 1633, the Right
Honourable <u>Ralph</u> <u>Freeman</u>: Neyther is it the least Honour to this
right Worshipfull Fraternity, that it pleased Royall King <u>James</u>, (of
sacred memory) besides divers others of the Nobility, to enter into
the freedome and brother-hood of this Company.

I come now to the first show by water which is a Sea-chariot,   <u>The first</u>
beautified and adorned with shel-fishes of sundry fashion and   <u>show by</u>
splendor, the Fabricke it selfe being visible to all, needeth not any <u>Water</u>
expression from me. This Chariot of no usuall forme or figure, is
drawne by two Griffons (the supporters to the Armes of the   120
Worshipfull Company): Those which ride upon these commixt Birds and
Beasts bearing staves with pendants falling from their tops, in which

58

are portray'd the Armes of the two Sheriffes now in place: The
speaker is Thamesis, or the Genius of the River Thames, increased to
this navigable depth by the meeting of the Tame and Isis, he being
seated in the front of the Chariot with his water Nymphes clad in
severall colours about him, seemeth asleepe, but at the approach of
the Lord Maiors Barge, he rowzeth himselfe as being newly wakend from
a Dreame, and speaketh as followeth.

            The Speech by Water.   130

      Can Thamesis himselfe so farre forget?
But 'tis so long since Tame and Isis met,
That 'tis not rare; for we two are growne old,
And being Rivers, subject to take cold;
Forc't with extremity of paine to grone,
As troubled with the gravell and the stone,   The River
Whole shelves are in our raines but (Fates so please) at this
By Artists helpe we late have got some ease.   time clin-
Thankes to our Patriots: O when I looke   ging by
On you, I must acknowledge to a Brooke   sundry
My River had beene turn'd, had not your care   water
Beene ever studious for our best well-fare.   engines.
(My recollection helpe me) you are hee
That up to Stanes and downe as farr as Lee,
Are my great Lord in cheife; first then I bow   To Stanes
To your Inauguration, and I now   upward and
Rowse me in my Sea Chariot, drawne or led   downe to
By your owne Griffons: Birds, who have the head   Lee, the
Of Eagles, Lyons body, wings beside,   Lord Maior
All Symboles of that Praetor, who shall guide   commandeth
So great a state; know further, Griffons can   the Thames.
Snatch from the Earth the harnest horse and man
To pray on them at pleasure, these imply
That you must alwayes have an Eagles eye
To out gaze the Sun, and keepe that Aquilant sight
To see what's wrong, and to distinguish right.

      The Lyons strength and boldnes you must have
(With all his pitty), for to such as crave
Or yeeld unto him, faining themselves dying,
Scorning to kil, he will not touch them lying: 160
But such as strike or shall oppugne his lawes,
He rends and teares them with his Kingly pawes.
The wings your Griffons beare, import what speede
Should be apply'd to such as justice neede:

      But why should I though best of Neptunes sonnes

59

(Whose streame almost by your permission runnes)
Instruct him who can teach? Since the last yeare
Till this day, never ran my Tides so cleare
As now they doe, were never so become
With Barges, Ensignes, Trumpets, Fyfe and Drum,   170
Me thinkes you make me yong againe to view
Old customes kept, and (in them) all things new.

        Though I by name of <u>Thamesis</u> ame knowne
My streames are yours, you welcome to your owne,
Passe, and returne safe, thus much on we build,
What's on my Waters wanting Land shall yeeld.

        The first Show by Land, presenteth it selfe in <u>Paules</u> Church-   <u>The first
yard</u>, which is a <u>Shepheard</u> grazing his flocke upon an Hill adorned   <u>Show by
with severall Trees, and sundry sorts of Flowers, he sitteth upon a   <u>Land</u>.
Dyall to which his sheepehooke is the <u>Gnomon</u>, (a Symbole of his care   180
and vigilancy,) upon the same plat-forme where his Sheepe are resting
in severall postures, appeareth a Woolfe ready to cease upon his
prey, at whose presence though his Dogge seeme terrified and flyes
for refuge to his master, yet he stands ready at all houres with a
bold spirit and wakefull eye, both for the defence of his charge and
offence of the comon adversary the Woolfe, which reflecteth upon the
office of the <u>Praetor</u> this day Inaugurated wherein is exprest, not
onely the care he ought to have of his flocke, but of the profit also
which ariseth from the fleece, from which the mistery of the Cloath-
Workers deriveth its Originall. <u>Pastor</u> or <u>Opilio</u> in the Roman   190
tongue, and in ours a <u>Shepheard</u>: the Hebrues call <u>Roheh</u>, from which
some are of opinion <u>Rex</u> and <u>Roy</u> are derived, the <u>Greekes</u> call him
<u>Poimin</u>, which properly implyes <u>Ovium</u> <u>pastor</u> or a feeder of Sheepe:
to which charge none ought to aspire who is not lawfully called, but
this Shepheard entereth by the Dore which is the voyce of a free
election, and is not that <u>Mercinarius</u> <u>pastor</u> of whom it is thus
spoken, <u>Hee seeth the Woolfe comming, and leaveth the Sheepe and
fleeth</u>, &c. I shall not neede to swell my pages by reciting the
sundry profits and emoluments arising from this most necessary
Mistery, without which no Common-Weale were able to subsist, nor to   200
reckon up into how many severall Provinces and Countries this
commodity of Cloath is transported and vended, nor what severall
sorts of wares (by barter, and commerce) are in exchange of that
brought over into our owne Kingdome; therefore to cut of
circumstance, I proceede to the Shepheards Speech as followeth.

60

The <u>Shepheards</u> Speech.

  If a true <u>Shepheard</u> you desire to see,
Looke this way, for hee's embleam'd here in me:
But you grave <u>Praetor</u> rais'd to this high state,
Hee whom as now I only personate   210
The numerous throng, which you this day behold
Are your owne Sheep, this Citty is their fold,
And by your grave descretion they shal best,
Know where to browze by day, by night to rest.

  As I, so you must on a <u>Diall</u> sit
Which hath no <u>Gnomon</u> but my staffe to it,
And such your <u>Swoord</u> is now, your wakefull eye
Must still be ope to watch where you can spy
The Ravenous <u>Woolfe</u> to presse, and block the way,
Least hee on any of your Flocke should prey: 220

  Although my Dog fly from him, who hath binne
Rent with his pawe, and feares his horrid grinne,
Yet at all houres (you see) I ready stand
With armed hart, and Sheepe-hooke in my hand,
(So with your Swoord must you) both with an hye
Undaunted Spirit, and with a Vigilant eye,
Least any envious thorne, or schratching bryer,
May race their Skinnes, or on their Fleeces tyer,
And that your charge so carefully be borne
They may be never <u>But</u> <u>in</u> <u>Season</u> shorne: 230

  Great reason too you have, for by this Trade,
(Of which Great <u>Freeman</u>, you first Free were made)
The whole Land's Cloath, no Mistery, no Art,
Science, or Manifacture, that hath part
In <u>Theory</u> or <u>Practick</u>, but must all
Give due respect to this in generall:
For since the Trade of Cloathing first begun,
Both from the scorching of the sommers Sun,
And blustering North-Winds, Rich, Poore, Young and Old
Have beene defenc'd, nor could that Fleece of Gold   240
<u>Colchos</u> still boasts, (in the Auncient Poets read)
So usefull proove, or make so fine a threed
With ours, (low pris'd because not counted rare)
No remote Climat's able to compare:
It is that onely Marchandize which brings
All novels wanting heere, even forreigne Kings
Have thought themselves Rich Habited to have worne
Such Cloath as for the commonnesse we scorne,
Oh blesse then our increase, those that have been
I'th' Worlds remote parts, and strange Nations seene,   250

For want of Cloath find them goe naked there,
Yet men like us, and the same Image beare,
Make much Sir of your great Charge, 'tis not mine,
Y'are the true Shepheard, I my place resigne.

The second Show by Land, presented in the upper end of Cheape-
side, is a Ship most proper to the Trade of Merchant-adventurers:
neither know I whom more aptly to imploy as Pilot therein then
Mercury, whom the Poets feigne not onely to the Diactorus, or
Internuntius betwixt the gods and men: as also the Leader of the
Graces, the Inventer of Wrestling, the Deviser of Letters, the Patron
of Eloquence, &c. (From whence hee hath sundry attributes and
denominations conferr'd upon him) but he is also termed the god of
Barter, buying, selling, and commerce in all Merchandise whatsoever.

The second Show by Land.

260

Wee reade of two onely imployed by the gods in Embassie unto men,
namely Iris and Mercury: The difference betwixt their imployments
is, that Iris for the most part commanded by Juno, (as being her
chiefe Attendant) and never by the rest of the gods, unlesse to fore-
tell Warre, Famine, Pestilence, or some strange Disaster: And
Mercury was negotiated but in sports, pastimes, marriage Feasts,
sollemne meetings, Showes, Ovations, Triumphs, spectacles of the like
nature, and therefore more proper to this Dayes imployment. He is
figured like a young man, fresh coloured and beardlesse: In his
right hand holding a Golden Purse, in his left a Caduzcaeus, (a Rod
with two Snakes twined and internoded about it,) their Heads meeting
at the top, and their Tayles at the bottome, which the AEgyptians
held to be an Embleame of Peace: and in ancient dayes Great men
imployde in the affaires of State, or forreigne Embassies, boare such
Staves, from whence they were called Caducaeatores: Hee weares Wings
upon his Hat and Heeles, intimating his Celerity: and behinde him
stands a Cocke, denoting his Vigilancy: so much for the person, I
come now to his Speech.

270

280

Mercuries Speech

I Mercury, the Patrone of all Trade,
Of Trafficke and Commerce, am this day made
A speaker from the Gods: (for my quicke motion
Can sayle as well upon the Land as Ocean):
And who the Merchant better can assure,
Then Mercury, the Lord of Mercature?

To you, this Day with state and power indow'd,
Whose winged Ships all forreigne Seas have plow'd,
And mauger, surge, gust, or tempestuous flawe

Bowing to the Lord Maior.

62

Discovered what our Pole-starre never saw.
They from cold Arctos to the burning Zone
Have washt their keeles to find out lands unknowne.
Crossing the Boreal and the Australl lynes,
To view the set and rise of all the Signes.
To you whose Factors in both Indies lye,
The East and West: (all parts both farre and nye,)
Who sometimes up, then downe the Volga steere,
To know in Musco what is cheape or deere:
And what Hesperian Tagus can affoord,
(To enrich this noble Island) takes aboord.
There's nothing the brave Persian can hold rare,
But hither brought by your great Cost and Care.
The potent Turke (although in faith adverse)
Is proud that he with England can commerce.
What Genoua, Luca, Florence, Naples, yeeldes,
What growes, or's found through all the Latian fields.
What is in China, Greece, or Ormous sold,
(That Diamond worthy to be set in Gold.)
For Norway, Danske, France, Spaine, the Netherlands,
What's best in them, comes frequent to our hands.
And for transportage of some surplus ware,
Our owne wants furnisht what we best can spare.
No rarity for profit or for pleasure,
But brought to us in an abundant measure.

    To this brave Isle, (by Neptune moated round)
You give a Wall; not fixt on any ground,
But moving 'tweene the Ocean and the Ayre,
Which as you build, so yearely you repayre.
And (though a woodden Fabricke) so well knit,
That should invasive force once menace it
With loud-voic't Thunder, mixt with Sulpherous flame,
'Twould sinke, or send them backe with feare and shame,
Grave Sir, no other president you neede
To follow now, then him whom you succeede:
Next on your Motto thinke: so happy proove,
Let your trust be in him that reignes above.

    The third Show by Land, is a Modell devised for sport to humour
the throng, who come rather to see then to heare: And without some
such intruded Anti-maske, many who carry their eares in their eyes,
will not sticke to say, I will not give a pinne for the Show. Since
therefore it consists onely in motion, agitation and action, and
these (expressed to the life) being apparently visible to all, in
vaine should I imploy a speaker, where I presuppose all his words
would be drown'd in noyse and laughter, I therefore passe to the
fourth and last.

Virginia,
New England,
the Bromoo-
thos and
St. Chri-
stof. are
parts of
the West-
Indies.

310

320

Compa-
nies Motto
My trust is
in God
alone.

The third
Show by
Land.

Which is a curious and neately framed Architecture, beautified with many proper and becomming Ornaments: bearing the Title of The Bower of Blisse. An Embleame of that future Happinesse, which not onely all just and upright Magistrates, but every good man, of what condition or quality soever in the course of his life, especially aimeth at: I dwell not on the description thereof, I will onely illustrate the purpose for the which it was intended: This Pageant is adorned with foure persons, which represent the foure Cardinall Vertues, which are behoovefull unto all who enter into any eminent place or Office. Prudence, Temperance, Justice, and Fortitude, which are so concatinated amongst themselves that the one cannot subsist without the other.

The fourth Show by Land.

The first Prudence, reformeth Abuses past, ordreth affaires present, and fore-seeth dangers future: Further (as Cicero observes) Justice without Prudence is resolv'd into Cruelty, Temperance into Fury, Fortitude into Tyranny. 350

Next Temperance, which as Hermes sayth, is Rich in losses, Confident in perills, Prudent in assaults, and happy in it selfe. As a man cannot be Temporate unlesse he be Prudent, so none can be truely valiant unlesse he be Temperate, neyther can Justice exist without Temperance, since no man can be truely just, who hath not his brest free from all purturbations.

Then Justice (which according to Cicero) is the badge of Vertue, the staffe of Peace, the maintenance of Honour. Moreover, Justice and Order are the preservers of the Worlds peace, the just Magistrate is in his word Faithfull, in his thought sincere, in his heart Upright, without feare of any but God and his Prince, without hate of any but the wicked and irregular. 360

Last Fortitude, which (as Epictetus observes) is the companion of Justice, and never contendeth but in Righteous Actions, it contemneth Perill, despiseth Calamities, and conquers Death, briefely Fortitude without Prudence is but Rashnes, Prudence without Justice is but Craftines, Justice without Temperance but Tyrany, Temperance without Fortitude but Folly. 370

Amongst the rest of the Persons placed in this structure, are the three Theologicall Vertues, Faith, Hope, and Charity, as hand-maides attending to conduct all such pious and religious Magistrates, the way to the caelestiall Bower of Blisse, (of which this is but a meere representation and signe) who ayme at that Glorious Place, least they anyway deviate from the true path that leadeth unto it. I proceede to the Speech.

64

<u>Prudence</u> the Speaker

    Grave <u>Praetor</u>, with your <u>Censors</u>, (Sheriffes elected,   380
And now in <u>place</u>) it is from you expected,
That having your Authority from Kings,
(And many hundred yeares since) all such things
As <u>Custome</u> (by <u>Time</u> strengthned) hath made good,
You should maintaine, withall your livelyhood,
Which that you will performe, we doubt the lesse.
When we consider who's your patronesse,
The <u>Holy</u> <u>and</u> <u>Blest</u> <u>Virgin</u>, (further) this
<u>Fabricke</u> before you plac't, <u>The</u> <u>Bower</u> <u>of</u> <u>blisse</u>.

    If we to greater, lesse things may compare   390
These present, but the petty <u>Symbols</u> are
Of what is future; for bare <u>Prudence</u> here
Pent and confin'd in humane <u>knowledge</u>, there
Shall be reduc't to <u>Wisedome</u> that's Divine.
<u>Temperance</u> (which is bare <u>Abstinence</u>) shall shine
In clarity immaculate: <u>Justice</u>, which
Oft swayes the Ballance so, that to the Rich
It most inclines, shall by an equall Scale,
(Leaning nor this, nor that way) so prevaile,
That <u>Right</u> in glorious Star-wreaths shalbe crown'd,   400
And <u>Injury</u> in tenebrous <u>Lethe</u> drownd.
Brave <u>Fortitude</u> which chiefely doth subsist
In opposition of the <u>Antigonist</u>.
(Whether that hee the Bodies mortall state
Seeke to supplant, or Soule insidiate)
Shall stand impugnable, and thenceforth be
Fin'd and repur'd to all Eternity:
When you arrive at yon Caelestiall Tower,
Which aptly may be titled <u>Freemans</u> <u>Bower</u>.

    The way to finde which, through these vertues lies   410
Call'd <u>Cardinall</u>: The stepps by which to rise,
These <u>Graces</u> shewe, <u>Faith</u>, <u>Hope</u> and <u>Love</u> attend you:
Who on their unseene wings shall soone ascend you.
These (when all Earths pompe failes) your prayers shal bring
Where Saints and Angels <u>Haleluiahs</u> sing.

    I cannot without just taxation of ingratitude, omit to speake
something of this Worshipfull company of the <u>Cloath-Workers</u>, at whose
sole charge the Tryumphs of this day were celebrated, for the <u>Master</u>,
the <u>Wardens</u> and the <u>Committi</u>, chosen to see all things accomodated
for this busines then in motion, I cannot but much commend both for   420
their affabillity and courtesie, especially unto my selfe being at
that time to them all a meere stranger, who when I read my (then

unperfect) Papers, were as able to judge of them, as attentively to heare them, and rather judicially considering all things, then nicely carping at any thing, as willing to have them furthered for his honour, to whom they are dedicate, as carefull to see them performed to their owne reputation and credit, in both which, there was wanting in them neyther incouragement nor bounty: and as they were unwilling in any vaine glory to shew new presidents to such that should succeede them, so they were loath out of parsimony to come short of   430
any who went before them, lesse I could not speake in modesty, and more I forbeare to utter least I might incurre the imputation of flattery, I come now to the twelve celestiall Signes, which may aptly be applied unto the twelve Moneths during the Lord Mayors government.

The Speech at Night.

Sleepe may you soundly Sir, tomorrow prest
To a yeares trouble for this one nights rest,
In which may Starres and Planits all conspire,
To warme you so by their celestiall Fire
Aries whose Gold-Fleece Greece doth so renowne   440
May both inrich you and this Glorious Towne,
That Taurus in your strength may so appeare,
You this great weight may on your Shoulders beare:
That the two Twins the Mothers blest increase,   Gemini.
May in this Citty still continue peace.
That Cancer who incites to hate and spleene
May not in your faire Government be seene
That Leo waiting on your judgement seate
May moderate his rage and scorching heate,
That the Celestiall Maide may you advice   Virgo.
Virgins and Orphans still to patronize
And rather then your justice heere should faile,
Libra no more be seene with Golden scale
And that the Scorpions sting may be so charm'd
The poore may not be wrong'd, nor innocent harm'd,   Sagittarius.
That Chirons bent bow so may guide your will,
You may still aime, but never shoot to kill:
And Capricorne though all things said to dare
Though he have power, yet may have will to spare
That as Aquarius doth his water power   460
You may your goodnes on this Citty shower,
Pisces, the last of Twelve, the Feete they guide
From Head to Foot, O may you so provide.

I conclude with the excellent Artist Mr. Gerald Chrismas, whose worth being not to be questioned (as a prime Master in his

66

profession,) I am of opinion that there is not any about the towne
who can goe beyond him, of whom I may boldly speake, that as Art is
an helpe to nature, so his experience is, and hath beene an extention
to the tryall and perfection of Art, therefore let every man in his
way strive to be eminent, according to that of Ovid. 2 De pont.   470
            Artibus ingenuis quaesita est gloria multis.

                          FINIS.

Textual Notes

Heywood's 1633 Lord Mayor's Show, Londini Emporia (Greg, Bibliography, no. 483; STC 13348) is extant in only one copy, located in the Huntington Library. A. M. Clark edits the text in the Luttrell Society publication, cited for the previous pageant text. I have adopted Clark's reconstructions of the cropped margins and used them in my edition.

Collation

(title page) Maioralty] Maiorty Q

159 faining] aining Q

241 the] the' Q

250 th'] th Q

338 curious] cutious Q

338 Architecture] Architect Q

367 Righteous] Rrighteous Q

370 Temperance] Temperancs Q

370 Justice] Juststice Q

443 weight] wieght Q

Commentary Notes

Sir Ralph Freeman, Clothworker, was inaugurated as the new mayor. This was Heywood's only pageant written for the Clothworkers. Vicenzo Gussoni again reports to the Venetian Senate: "The change of Mayor was celebrated with costly show and a numerous attendance in the usual way, he being the one who acts as a very important magistrate in this city. I took part by invitation, as ambassador of the most serene republic, at the head of the procession, the Dutch minister and the Lords of the royal Council taking their places behind mine" (CSP Venetian, XXIII, 163). Guild records include negotiation with Gerard Christmas and a payment of £140 for the pageants (Collections V, pp. 12-13).

20-21 Lyvi. Decad. Lib. 4. Gratia & honos opportuniories interdum non cupientibus sunt] Book IV, section lvii, lines 3-10, "favour and high office sometimes come more easily when men do not covet them."

26-27 Semper honos nomenque suum laudesque manebunt] from Virgil, Aeneid, 1. 610: "Always his honor, his name, and his praises will endure."

31-32 Seneca, Bonum est laudari . . . laudabilem] "It is good to be praised but more excellent to be praiseworthy." Again, not to be found in Seneca.

49-50 (for so sayth Plutarch in Solon) . . . according to Aristotle] Plutarch, perhaps sec. xxii of Solon; Aristotle, perhaps Book II of the Politics.

64-65 Plato sayth . . . the least] a possible reference to Plato's Apology; this is a leading theme of that dialogue. See 2362-23 of that dialogue: "This man among you, mortals, is wisest who, like Socrates, understands that his wisdom is worthless" (tr. Grube).

66-67 Wee reade also in Socrates] the association of young men with desire and excess (hybris) is typical throughout Greek literature.

76-77 Heavenly treasure . . . Sea wracke] a paraphrase of Matthew 6: 19-21.

106-112 William Hart . . . Ralph Freeman] William Hart [Hewet], first Clothworker mayor; wealthy merchant, lived on London Bridge; his only daughter was rescued and later married by Edward Osborne when she fell from the Bridge. Rowland Hayward [or Heyward], sheriff 1563; son of George Hayward; died December 1593. James Howell [Hawes], sheriff 1567; son of Thomas of London; died 1582. Edward Osborne, saved Hart's daughter; ancestor of the Dukes of Leeds; became Vicount Dunblaine for his financial support of James I. Thomas Skinner, arrested in 1589 by order of the Queen in Council for withdrawing from London without contributing to the forced loan in spite of his fellow aldermen's attempts to make him comply. John Spencer, caused the companies to lay in supplies of corn during a time of great scarcity; suppressed with severity several tumultuous meetings of apprentices and others. Michael Moseley, [Nicholas Moseley], sheriff 1590; son of Edward of Hough, Cheshire; Alderman of Aldersgate for five years. John Watts, son of Thomas of Buntingford, Herts., was born about 1550; Alderman of Aldersgate for eight years beginning 1594; sheriff 1596; during his mayoralty he entertained James I; died 1616. Ralph Freeman, sheriff 1623; Alderman of Cornhill; son of William of Northampton; died in office March 1634.

113-115 King James . . . this Company] see the account in Nichols, Progresses of King James, II, 132, based on Howes in which the events are described that took place on 12 June 1607 while Watts was mayor.

120 two Griffons] as Heywood correctly notes these animals constitute the supporters to the arms of the Clothworkers as indicated in the patent of arms in 1587 (see Bromley, Armorial Bearings, p. 46). The arms are reproduced on the quarto title page.

180 the Gnomon] the rod that casts a shadow to indicate the time of the day. The tableau of the shepherd obviously alludes to the guild.

197-198 Hee seeth . . . fleeth] another biblical allusion, this to John 10: 12.

240 Fleece of Gold] reference to the story of Jason, perhaps prompted for Heywood by the golden ram on the blazon of the Clothworkers' crest.

246 novels] news, findings (OED).

258-260 Mercury . . . the Leader of the Graces] a common Renaissance idea as shown in Edgar Wind's Pagan Mysteries in the Renaissance. Botticelli's Primavera is a good example from Renaissance art.

280 a Cocke] this may be Heywood's invention. In the 1619 Lord Mayor's Show, The Triumphs of Love and Antiquity, Middleton has Orpheus accompanied by a cock, signifiying the vigilancy the magistrate must maintain.

291 mauger] ill-will, spite (OED).

297 Factors] a doer, agent (OED).

309 Ormous] (Ormuz) island off of South Iran, captured by the Persian-English forces in 1622 from the Portuguese.

328 Let your trust . . . above] a variation of the Clothworkers' motto: "My trust is in God above"

70

331 Anti-maske] the first time that a pageant dramatist has used this term in a printed text of a street entertainment. Heywood adopts the term from the court masque.

338 Architecture] though the text reads "Architect," the OED shows no meaning that would be appropriate; therefore, it has been emended to "Architecture," a structure or building. See 1. 385 in the 1637 pageant text.

351-53 Cicero observes Justice without Prudence . . . Tyranny] Heywood seems to have in mind Cicero's De Officiis, especially the long discussion on Justice in Book I, particularly chapters 7-13.

360 Justice (which according to Cicero)] again Heywood probably intends Cicero's De Officiis; indeed, Cicero discusses at some length the Cardinal Virtues, especially in Book I.

366 Fortitude, which (as Epictetus observes)] perhaps Book I, chapters 28, 29, 30.

388 Holy and Blest Virgin] Heywood seems to have confused the patroness of the Drapers for the Clothworkers' presumed patroness. I find no evidence that the Virgin was also patroness of the Clothworkers.

405 insidiate] to lie in wait for, plot against (OED).

412 These Graces] the first of Heywood's many references to the Theological Virtues: Faith, Hope, and Love, based on 1 Corinthians 13: 1-13.

416-433 I cannot . . . flattery] Heywood outdoes himself in praising the cooperation and undertanding of the guild. This was his only time to write for the Clothworkers. Despite such heady praise, the Clothmakers chose John Taylor to write their 1634 pageant.

450 advice] an acceptable spelling for the verb "advise," which is what Heywood means.

464 Gerald Chrismas] though Heywood cannot seem to decide how to spell the artificer's name, he consistently praises Christmas' artistry.

470-471 Ovid. 2 De pont. Artibus . . . multis] Ovid in Ex Ponto, II. vii. 47, "By liberal arts many have sought renown."

Londini Sinus Salutis,

or,

LONDONS Harbour of Health,

and Happinesse.

Expressed in sundry Triumphs, Pageants

and Showes; at the Initiation of the

Right Honorable,

CHRISTOPHER CLETHROWE,

Into the Maioralty of the farre Renowned

City LONDON.

All the Charges and Expences of this present

Ovation being the sole undertaking of the Right

Worshipfull Company of the

Ironmongers.

The 29. of October. Anno Salutis. 1635.

Written by THOMAS HEYWOOD.

Redeunt Spectacula.

Printed at London by Robert Raworth. 1635.

73

                        To the Right
            Honorable, Christopher Clethrowe,
              Lord Maior of this Renowned
                Metropolis, LONDON.

    Right Honorable,
    It is one of Erasmus his undeniable Apothegms, that there is no
Citie can bee so strongly immur'd or Defenc'd, but may bee either by
Engins defaced, by Enemies invaded, or by Treason surprized; but the
Counsells and Decrees of a wise Magistrate, are in-expugnable. Time,
and your Merit, have call'd you to this Office and Honor: As all   10
eyes are upon you, so all hearts are towards you; never was any more
freely voyc't in his Election, and therfore none more hopefull in
expectation: your Abilitie, what you can doe, is knowne; your
purpose, what you intend, you have amply delivered; onely the
Performance remaines: In which, there is no question, but that you
will accommodate all your future Proceedings to these three heads:
Pro Rege, pro Lege, pro Grege; for as you are a Magistrate, so you
are a Judge: A calling, both of Trust, and Trouble: Of Trust;
because all such as sit in Judicature, are Persons ordained by God,
to examine Causes discreetely; Heare both Parties Considerately, and   20
Censure all matters unpartially: For Justice is the Badge of Vertue,
the staffe of Peace, and the maintainance of Honor. Of Trouble;
because in no part of your Time, during your regency, neither is
publicke, or private, forraine, or domestick things, whether you
meditate alone, or converse with others, you shall find the least
vacancie, which remembers me of that which Dion witnesseth of one
Similis, who living long in great Place and Authoritie under the
Emperour Adrian, after much intreaty, got leave to retire himselfe
into the Countrey, where after seaven contented yeeres expiring, hee
caused this Epitaph to be Insculpt upon his tombe: Similis hic   30
jacet, cujus aetas multorum fuit annorum. Septem tamen Duntaxat,
Annos vixit. Lanctantius further teacheth us, that it is most
requisite, in all such as have charge in the Common Weale, under
their Prince and Governour, so to know the bownds of their Calling,
and understand the full effects of their dutie, that by executing
Justice, they may be feared, and by shewing Mercy, bee loved: I
conclude all in this short sentence, Non, quid Ipse velis, sed quod
lex & Religio Cogat, Cogita, Ever submitting my selfe to your better
Judgement, and remaining, to your Lordship most obsequious,

                        Thomas Heywood.   40

LONDONS
SINUS SALUTIS.

I shall not neede to borrow my Induction from the Antiquitie of
this Famous Metropolis, nor to enter into a large discourse, of the
noble Magistracy and government thereof; being Arguments already
granted, and therefore unnecessary to be disputed: and yet I hold it
not altogether Impertinent to remember some few things of remarke,
which have happened in the Praetorships of the Right Honourable, the
Lord Maiors of this Renowned Citie, who have beene Free of the Right
Worshipfull Company of the Iron-Mongers.   50

In the yeere 1409, Richard Marloe, of the same Fraternitie,
bearing the Sword, there was a Show presented by the Parish Clerkes
of London, at a place called Skinners Well, and now Clerken Well,
which was of matter from the Creation of the World; and lasted for
the space of Eight Intyre dayes: Edward the Fourth (then King) being
present with his Queene, and the greatest part of his Nobilitie,
which Richard Marloe, was after Inagurated into the same Honor, Anno
1417. In the yeere 1566, Sir Christopher Draper, being Lord Maior,
King James, of late and most Sacred memory, was borne the Sixth day
of June. Anno 1569, in Sir Alexander Avenons Maioralty, was the   60
suppression of the Rebells in the North. Anno 1581, Sir Francis
Harvey being Mayor, was the French Mounsiers comming over into
England, and his Royall entertainement by Queene Elizabeth. Anno
1609, Sir Thomas Cambel being Invested into the same Honor: All the
like Showes and Triumphs belonging unto the solemnitie of this day,
which for some yeeres, had beene omitted and neglected, were by a
speciall commandement from his Majestie, King James, againe retained,
and have beene till this present day continued; whom since hath
succeeded in the same Honor, Sir James Cambel, his Sonne, a worthy
Senator of this Citie, yet living, (The last of this worthy and   70
Worshipfull Company, who hath sate in that seate of Justice) now this
day succeeded by the Right Honourable, Christopher Clethrowe: but I
leave all circumstances, and come to the Showes, now in present
Agitation.

The first Showe by Water:

Is an Artificiall Moddell, partly fashioned like a Rock, and
beautified with sundry varieties, and rarities, in all which Art (in
Imitating) striveth to exceed Nature: The Decorements that adorne
the Structure, I omit, and descend to the Persons that furnish it,
which are the Three Caelestiall Goddesses, Juno, Pallas, Venus: In   80
Juno, is figured Power and State; In Pallas or Minerva, Arms and
Arts; In Venus, Beautie and Love: The first best knowne by her

Peacocks; the second by her Owles; the third by her Swans and
Turtles, who is also attended by her Sonne Cupid, in whom is Emblem'd
Love; by whom some have thought, the Universe to have beene Created,
because of the Beautie, Glory, and Flourishing forme thereof, as
also, that Love (though pictured young) yet in Age exceeds all
things: But Venus, because borne of the Seas, I hold most proper to
speake upon the Waters: These Three Goddesses are sent from Jupiter,
with severall Presents, to honour this dayes Triumphs, and him to   90
whom they are devoted; Juno brings Power, Pallas Wisedome, Venus
Love; whose Speech is as followeth:

Venus the Speaker.

    The Three Caelestiall goddesses this day
Descend (Grave Praetor) to prepare your way
To your new Oath, and Honor: Jove, whose station
Is still above, hath sent to this Ovation
And glorious Triumph, Us: Juno the great
And Potent Queene; who to your Jurall seat,
Brings State and Power: Pallas, who from Joves brain   100
Derives her selfe, and from the highest straine
Of all the other gods, claimes her descent,
Her Divine Wisedome, doth this day present.

    But I, Emergent Venus, Loves faire Queene,
Borne of the Seas, and therefore best beseene
To speake upon the Waters, bring a gift,
Priz'd equally with theirs; that which shall lift
You up on voyces, and from the low frame
Of sordid Earth, give you (above) a name:
From just affections, and pure thoughts, Love springs,   110
And these are Impt with no Icarian wings,
But Plumes Immortall, such as Angels beare,
To fixe your Name in an eternall spheare.

    Which to attaine; Take Juno for your guide,
Maintaine her Peacocks riches, not her pride;
Who to prove all Earths glory is but vaine,
Lookes but upon her feete, and flaggs her traine.

    Observe next Pallas Owles, and from them take
This notion; you must watch even as they wake:
For all such as the management of state   120
Shall undergoe, rise earlie, and bed late,
So Wisedome is begot; from Wisedome Love,
(Sweete Child of such a Parent) may't then prove:
That as this day you doe attract the eyes,

And expectation of the great, and wise,
So in the happy progresse of your yeere,
You may their hearts and soules to you Indeere:
    From Love, your Waters passage understand,
    But Power and Wisedome, wellcoms you on land.   130

    The next Modell by Land, which was onely showne upon the Water,
is one of the Twelve Caelestiall signes: Sagitarius called Croton;   Sagitarius.
hee, before hee was translated into the Heavens, was said to bee the
Sonne of Pan, and the Nimph Euphemes, and in his Infancy, was
Conlacteus Musarum. i. Hee suckt of the same brest with the Muses,
his mother being their Nurse, and dwelt in Helicon; hee was Famous
for his skill in Archerie, wonderous swift of foote, and when the
Nine Sisters sung to their severall instruments of Musick, his
custome was to dance before them in sundry active figures and
postures. For which, and other indowments, knowne to be eminent in,   140
hee was at their request to Jupiter translated amongst the starres;
in the plat-forme, on which hee is borne, at the foure corners, are
seated foure other dignified with the like Constellations: Virgo,   Virgo.
best knowne by the name of Astrea and Justa, the daughter of Jupiter,
and Themis; and for her Justice and Integritie, thither transferr'd,
and numbred amongst the Twelve: Next Ariadne, best knowne amongst   Ariadne.
the Astrologians, by the name of Corona, the Crowne, which was said
to bee forged by Vulcan in Lemnos, the materialls thereof were Gold,
and Indian Gemmes, of extraordinary splendor, which shee lending to
Theseus at that time when her Father Minos had expos'd him to the   150
Minotaure, by the luster thereof, hee passed freely through the
darknesse of the Laborinth: Some say, it was first given her by
Liberpater, or Bacchus, the Sonne of Jupiter and Semele, and was the
price of her Virginitie: but howsoever, shee being most ingratefully
forsaken by Theseus, in the Ile of Naxos, was there found by Bacchus,
who having espoused her with great solemnitie, caused her after her
death, with this Crowne to bee Invested in the Firmament. The Third,   Cassiopeia.
Cassiopeia, the wife of Cepheus, who preferring her owne beautie
before the Nereides, who were the daughters of Neptune, was for that   160
insolence, doom'd to be bownd in a chayre, hand and foote, and so
placed amongst the spheares, where shee remaines Conspicuous, in   Andromeda.
Thirteene Starres. The Fourth, is Andromeda, the Daughter of Cepheus
and Cassiopeia, who by the wrath of Neptune, being chain'd unto a
Rocke, and ready to bee devoured by a Sea Monster, was delivered
thence by Perseus, the Sonne of Jupiter, and Danaae, to whom being
after married, was call'd Persa, and Stellified by Minerva: The
Speaker is an Astrologian.

                The Speech followeth:

Late risen in the Heaven is Sagitary,

(With you, great Lord) who doth about him carry   170
Fifteene bright Starres, most Influent, and these all
Appearing in the Circle hiemall:
His Bow devided in that beaten roade,
Call'd Galaxia, where the gods have troade
So oft; that looke upon it in the night,
When all the rest's dull, that alone shines bright:
(As you now at this instant): Hee fifteene
Starres, did I say? How you then, who betweene
Your landing and repose, by power divine,
Have full Three-score, about your state to shine: 180
For every Company's a Starre this day,
Visible to all, and over these you sway:
But twelve in chiefe; and those wee must confesse,
Of greater lustere made, to guide the lesse:
All enjoy one like Freedome, all are Free,
And all (Great Praetor) to bee rul'd by thee:
Commanding all the rest, who in thy spheare,
Now rising, art to shine a compleate yeere.

    You may observe his Bow still ready bent,   190
In which there is a perfect Emblem ment
Of Divine Justice: Th' Arrow, with a Starre
Headed, implies, that her power reacheth farre;
And no opposure, fraude, violence, or rape,
Can (when shee aimes to strike) her vengeance scape;
Yet though the string be drawne up to his eare,
(As alwayes prest) hee rather seemes with feare
To threat, then punish, and though hee can still
Let loose his shafts, hee seldome shoots to kill.

    Observe it well, the Morrall doth imply,   200
All Justice should be mixt with lenitie,
So, imitate the gods, since them wee know,
Apt still to Mercie, but to vengeance slow:
And the Caelestiall bodies, though they trade
Above, yet were for our example made.
As oft as man sinnes, should Jove punnish vice,
His Quiver would be emptied in a trice,
And man-kind, at once perish: O mixe then
Mercy with Justice, Interweave againe
Justice with Mercy; so shall you in your state,
Not Starres alone, but the gods Imitate;   210
So shall your Terrene body, in the end,
All the Caelestiall bodies farre transcend,
And deckt with better lights then those you see
Above the spheares, shine to eternitie.

78

The Third Plat-forme, is contrived onely for Pastime, to please the vulgar, and therefore deserves no further Charractar, then a plaine nomination, as devised onely to please the eye, but no way to feast the eare: and so I leave it to proceede to the next.

The Fourth Moddell, is a Castle munified with sundry Peeces of Ordnance; and Accomodated with all such Persons as are needfull for the defence of such a Citadell: the Gunner being ready to give fire upon all occasions; as for the curious Art in the contriving thereof, I make no question but the worke it selfe is sufficiently able to commend the Worke-man, being knowne to be an excellent Artist, of which, the spectatours may best censure; I will onely deliver unto you a word or two concerning the presenter, which is Mars.

220

Hee is styled the third amongst the gods, because hee stands in that degree amongst the Planets: and is said to be the sonne of Jupiter; some write that Bellona was his Nursse, others that she was his Mother, and some his sister. Yet none of these improper, for Ennio which is Bellona, implies no more then an incouragement of the minde to hardinesse and valour in all Skyrmishes and Battailes. He is also cal'd Ares which signifieth Dammage or detriment, and Mavors quasi Mares vorans, of devouring of men; and by the Gentiles, had the Denomination of the god of Battailes. He was antiently figured an angry man sitting in a Chariot, armed with a sheild and other weapons, both offensive, and defensive: Upon his head a plumed Helmet, his sword mounted upon his thigh, hee held in one hand a whip, in the other, the Raines, being drawne in his Chariot by wylde and untam'd Horses. Before him was portraied a Wolfe devouring a Lambe, the Wolfe being the beast particularly offered upon his shrine, and because the two Romane Twinnes the first founders of Rome, Romulus and Remus, were fained to be the sonnes of Mars (of which the one slewe the other) therefore Romulus is figured upon his Chariot as the unnaturall survivor. The Athenians were the first that ever sacrificed to this god of Warre, which Celebration was call'd Ekaton pephomena for whosoever had slaine an Hundred of the publike Enemies, was bownd to sacrifice a man upon his Altar, situate in the Ile Lemnos, but after the bloodinesse, and inhumanitie thereof, displeasing the Athenians, they changed that custome, and in the stead of a man, offered a gelded Hogge, which they call'd Nefrendes: Varro writes, that amongst the Romans, Sicinnius Dentatus, having fought one hundered and Ten severall Duells, and being Victor in them all, receiving Forty five wounds, whose skarres were visible upon his body, all before, and none backward: Hee was for his Valour, honoured with Twenty five severall Crownes, and received moreover, an Hundred and Forty golden Bracelets; and was the first amongst the Romanes, that ever made oblation to this Deity: Mars sitting in the front of the Tower, speakes as followeth.

Mars.

230

His sundry Denomina-tions.

240

250

The Speech of Mars.

260

Bellipotent Mars is from his spheare come downe,
To heighten these brave Triumphs of Renowne,
Seated in this mur'd Citadel, defenc'd
With Bullets wrapt in Fire, and Cloudes condenst.

A Peece
goes off.

The Tormentary Art, not long since found,
Which shatters Towers, and by which Ships are drown'd,
I bring along; to let you understand
These guard your safety, both by Sea, and Land.

O, when I late saw from mine orbe Divine,
So many Sonnes of Mars, amongst you, shine
In compleat Arms, Plum'd Casks, and Ensigns spred
By such brave Captaines, and Commanders led:
No Souldier, but his Posture to the life,
Acting to th' Musick of the Drum and Fyffe,
Some practising small Bombards, some the great,
Whose very thunder, rows'd mee from my seate:
This Peacefull Citie, I much prays'd, whose power
Could to a Campe, it selfe change in an houre:
Proceed in your brave Practise; whil'st I tell
Wherein your Iron and Steele doth most excell.

270

280

Without these Metalls, Nature could produce
Nothing that is conducefull to mans use:
The Plow, without the Coulter and the Share,
Could make no Furrowes, and those Graines that are
Upon them throwne, were lost to them that sowe them,
Without the Sickle, and the Sythe to mowe them:
The Gardeners Art, would cease to be a trade,
If take from him the Matocke, and the Spade.
In Denns and Caves wee should be forc'd to dwell,
Were there no Axes made, that Timber fell:
Nor on the Seas could wee have Shipps to sayle,
Without the Sawe, the Hammer, and the Nayle:
Aske those that take in Angling most delight,
Without the baited Hooke, no fish will bite.
The Iron Crowe turnes up the Indian mould,
Trenching the Earth untill they dig out Gold.
If with the Iron the Adamant should contend,
There should be no more Compasse, but an end
Of all Discovery: Even the Horse wee ride
Unshod, would founder, who takes greatest pride,
When the most curb'd, and playing with the bit,

290

300

Hee snowes the ground, and doth the Spurre forgit.
There is no Art, Craft, Faculty, or Trade,
Without it, can subsist: Your Sword is made
Of these mixt Metalls (Sir). Justice would cease,
If (as in Warre) it were not us'd in Peace:
Power makes it yours, your wisedome now direct you;
Whilst Peace swayes heere, Mars shall abroad protect you.

  The speech being ended, the Ordnance goeth off from the Castle;
and now I come to the fift and last.   310

  Heere I might enter into large discourse, concerning the
commodiousnesse of Iron and Steele, and to speake of Tuball Cain, who
made the first Forge, and found out the use of these Metalls: as
also Vulcan the deified Smith and of his Cyclopean Hammers with which
hee was said to have beaten out Joves Thunder-boults, with other
fixions to the like purpose, these having before been exposed to the
publick view upon occasion of the like solemnity, and knowing withall
that Cibus bis coctus, relisheth not the quesie stomackes of these
times, I therefore purposly omit them proceeding to the last
Pageants, styled Sinus salutis, first the Boosome, or harbour of   320
Health and Happinesse. The sculpture being adorned with eight
several persons, representing such vertues as are necessary to bee
imbraced by all such Majestrates, who after their stormy and
tempestuous progresse through all judicature causes incident to their
places, seeke to anchor in that safe and secure Port so styled.

  Every Magistrate is a minister under God, appointed by his divine
ordinance to that calling, to be a protector of the Church, a
preserver of discipline and Peace, consonant with his lawes, the
lawes of nature, and the land, which hee ought faithfully to execute
with corporall punishment, correcting the proud and disobedient, and   330
against all unjust oppressors, defending the conformable and humble.
The first vertue adorning the structure is stiled Fortitudo togata,   Fortitudo
which gowned Fortitude is thus defined.   togata.

  A constancy of minde persevering in honest purpose rightly
undertaken and according to his place and calling, tollerating
private injuries for lawdable causes, dispising pleasures, corrupt
guifts, detraction, and the like: and these meerly for vertues sake
and preferring the publike good before his owne private gaine, &c.
Of which Fabritius was a noble president, who refusing the gold sent
him by Pyrhus was no whit affrighted with the terror of his   340
Elephants; to speake or act any thing against the dignity of the
Republicke. Of whom Eutropius reports Pyrhus to have said: the
Sunne is more easie to bee altered in his course, then this Fabritius
to be removed from his honesty.

Mansuetudo, or gentlenesse is a vertue mediating wrath and suppressing all desire of revenge and remitting offences, for publicke concords sake, which notably appeared in Pericles, who when one had bitterly rayled on him, for space of one whole afternoone in the open market place: night comming, hee caused his servants to light him to his house with Torches.

Candor, or sincerity is when without simulation we our selves speake, and with no diffidence suspect the good meaning of others: wishing all just men well, rejoycing at theire prosperity, and commisserating their disaster: It is reported of Trajanus the Emperour, that when Sura Licinius one of the Tribunes, was accused unto him, to have Insidiated his life, not questioning the faith of so knowne a friend; the same night, un-invited, supt with him privately in his house, and the Table being with-drawne, trusted himselfe to be trim'd by Sura's Barbar.

Patientia Philosophica, is a Vertue obedient unto reason, in bearing wrongs, and suffering adversities; it moderates griefe, and bridles nature, so that it never rebells against Justice, Modesty, Constancy, or any other vertue; Xenophon reports Cyrus and Agesolanus, to be of such Philosophical patience, that in their height of determination in all their actions, and speech, they appeared to all men affable, and offencelesse.

Placabilitie is a vertue, having correspondence with that which I before stil'd Mansuetudo, or Gentlenesse; Philosuchia, or study of Peace, and Concord, is when a Magistrate thinks Humbly of himselfe, moderating his owne anger, and bearing with the Infirmities of others, pardoning Injuries, and maintaining unitie, being provident that all unnecessary controversie bee aton'd, least the publike Peace and Unitie of the Church, or Common-weale be disturbed, or hindred; of which Vertue, Abraham was a most Imitable President, who, though in Authoritie, Wisedome, and age, hee had Prioritie before Lot, yet not-with-standing, gave place to him; only for Concords sake.

Humanitie, which the Greekes call Ethos, is Justice, coupled with Gentlenesse, Equitie, Upright-life, Affabilitie, and the like, for which are remark't, Alexander, Cyrus, Octavius Caesar, &c. It hath also beene observed amongst Schollars (in which number I may Catalogue your Lordship), that the more learned they have beene, they have shewed themselves the more humane, and humble.

The last is Nemesis, or Zeale, which is an ardent love of Gods glory, of Justice, Pietie, Sanctitie, &c. With an earnest Indignation against whatsoever is evill, supporting the Religious, and severely punishing the wicked, and refractory: Phinees zelo Inflammatus Confodit scortatorem, &c. So much to Illustrate the Persons; I come now to the Speech.

Mansuetudo. 350

Candor.

Patientia Phylosophica.

Placabilitas. 370

Humanitas. 380

Nemesis sive Zealus.

Hee that is call'd to bee a Majestrate,   390
A Guide, a Ruler, or a Candidate,
Must of so great a burden know the weight;
But first the stepps that mount him to that height:
Shall I direct you then, what sayle to beare?
(Like a good Pilot) and what course to steare:
(Your pardon, Great Sir) daring to descry
A passage, which you better know then I.

There is double Fortitude, both Crown'd
With merited Palme; one Gunn'd, the other Gown'd:
The Souldier claymes the first, as his by due,   400
The next, the Civill Sword, now borne by you:
By which, as great a glory you shall win
In Peace, as hee in Warre, by curbing sinne,
And cherishing vertue; In the second place,
Stands Gentlenesse, and Mercy, O what grace
Hath Peace, with Pitty mixt? Metalls best feele,
When Iron is well Incorporate with Steele:
A body so calcin'd to publike use,
As to support Right, and suppresse abuse:
Sinceritie may chalenge the third classe,
Next Patience, which by suffering, doth surpasse   410
All other Vertues: Placability,
Study of Concord, and Fidelity;
Last, holy Zeale, and that doth crowne the rest:
All these being harbour'd in your honour'd brest,
Shall (maugre shelves and rocks) your passage cleare,
And bring you to the Port, to which you steare:
You are the Cities Chiefe, the Prime, the Sole,
In expectation: like the stedfast Pole:
Proove constant in your Course be still the same,
So let your Sword (tutch'd with Truth's Adamant) aime   420
In your yeeres compasse, that to all mens view
(Skilfull in stearage) it may still goe true:
     So, those that were before you, and rul'd well,
     Equall you shall, although not Antecell.

There remaines the Speech at Night, which is onely a Summary, or
reiteration of the former Showes, Applied to the taking leave of his
Lordship, and to commend him to his rest: Mars being the Speaker.

The Speech at Night.

Phoebus his Steedes hath stabled in the West,   430
And Night (succeeding Day) invites to rest:
The Three Caelestiall Queenes, sent from above,

Leaving with you their Power, their Wisdom, Love
Now take their leaves: The Centaure doth bestow
On you his Justice, with his shaft, and bowe,
Who to your best repose, bequeath's you heere,
To mount himselfe againe unto his spheare:
The Night being come, he cannot well be mist;
For without him, his Orbe cannot subsist:
Neither can mine: Now must my Starre display
Its Luminous Rays, being borrowed thence this day,   440
To waite upon your Triumphs, and shall still
Protect you, and your weighty charge, untill
Hee, which shall all your upright Actions blesse,
Conduct you to your Port of Happinesse.

　　These Frames, Modells, and Structures, were Fashioned, Wrought,
and Perfected, by the Two Artists, John, and Mathias Chrismas;
Successors to their Father, Mr. Gerald Chrismas, late disceased, as
well in the Exquisite performance of his qualitie, as in his true
sincerite, and honesty; of whom I may confidently speake, as no man
could out-vie him in these Workes, which hee underwent, so none could   450
out-match him in his word, for any thing hee undertooke; concerning
whom I make no scruple, thus Ingeniously to conclude: Ars Patris, in
filiis etiam, post fata viget.

　　　　　　F I N I S.

84

Textual Notes

This 1635 Lord Mayor's Show, Londini Sinus Salutis (Greg, Bibliography, no. 500; STC 13348a), was printed by Robert Raworth and is the only Heywood pageant not printed by the Okes shop, either Nicholas or John. This is also the only Heywood pageant text printed in an octavo format rather than quarto. The one extant copy is in the Dyce Collection of the Victoria and Albert Museum. An edition of this pageant appears in the 1874 edition of Heywood, volume 4. I have accepted that editor's version of the cropped margins.

Collation

(title page) Expressed] 1874; Epressed 8°

  16 your] year 1874

  58 1566,] 1566. 8°, 1874

  60 1569,] 1569. 8°, 1874

  61 1581,] 1581. 8°, 1874

  64 1609,] 1607. 8°, 1874

  83 Peacocks] 1874; Peacoeks 8°

133 hee] he 1874

142 borne,] borne: 8°, 1874

157 Firmament] 1874; Frmament 8°

207 then] them 1874

251 the] omitted, 1874

274 th'] 'th 8°, 1874

319 times,] times. 8°, 1874

329 execute] 1874; excecute 8°

335 undertaken] 1874; unertaken 8°

336 injuries] 1874; jnjuries 8°

336 causes] cause 1874

356 unto] 1874; nnto 8°

363 reports] ports 1874

379 Octavius] 1874; Octavus 8°

383 (margin) Nemesis] 1874; Nenesis 8°

425 Summary] Sumnary 8°, 1874

440 Its] It's 8°, 1874

Commentary Notes

For a total expenditure of £550. 10s. 9d, the Ironmongers
celebrated the inauguration of Sir Christopher Cletherow, as mayor.
Guild records show very revealingly that John Christmas and Heywood
successfully underbid Robert Norman and John Taylor--Taylor had
written the 1634 pageant for the Clothworkers. Norman and Taylor
insisted on a payment of £190, but Heywood and Christmas were
offering their services for £180. In addition to the pageant devices
that they would provide, they also promised "to give the Company 500
bookes of the declaracion of the said Shewe. Which offer the Courte
accepted & agreed therunto" (Collections, p. 123). Norman and Taylor
were given a consolation payment. Guild records are full of many
kinds of payments. Heywood and Christmas essentially provided
everything necessary for the pageant itself. The Venetian
Ambassador, this time Anzolo Correr, was again present and dispatched
this report: "The election of the new Mayor of London was celebrated
yesterday with the usual rejoicings. I took part in the function, as
is usual, having been invited with the other ambassadors" (CSP Ven,
XXIII, 475).

2 Christopher Clethrowe] sheriff 1625, son of Henry of
   London; president of Christ's Hospital; died 1641.

6 Erasmus his undeniable Apothegms] the closest parallel to
   what Heywood reports of Erasmus is the following statement
   found in Erasmus: "For a castle, or any stronghold is not
   so sure and safe from enemies, by the sense of diches and
   walles, as by valiaunte and hardie mennes bodies"
   (Apophthegemes of Erasmus).

26-27 Dion witnesseth . . . Similis] this incident of
   Similis is recorded in Cassius Dio Cocceinus, History of
   Rome, Book LXIX, including the inscription on the tomb
   referred to by Heywood, which translates: "Here lies
   Similis, who existed so-and-so many years, and lived seven."

86

32 Lanctantius further teacheth us. . .] the "Christian
    Cicero" appointed by Constantine to educate the Prince
    Crispus in Gaul, writes in his Divinae Institutiones on the
    nature of justice in Book V, especially chapter xv. He
    writes at one point: ". . . no one is most renowned, but he
    who has abundantly performed works of mercy; no one is
    perfect, but he who has filled all the steps of virtue."

37-38 Non, quid Ipse velis, sed quod lex & Religio Cogat,
    Cogita] "Not what you yourself want, but what law and
    relgion compel."

51 Richard Marloe] [Merlawe], Ironmonger, sheriff 1402,
    Lord Mayor 1409 and 1417; Alderman Queenhithe; MP from
    London several times; died 1420.

51-56 In the yeere 1409 . . . Edward the Fourth . . . being
    present] As Stow writes in his Annales (1615 ed.): "This
    yeere was a great play at the Skinners well, neere unto
    Clearken-well besides London, which lasted eight dayes, and
    was of matter from the creation of the world . . ." (p.
    337). It is doubtful that Edward IV was present, as Heywood
    says, since he was not yet born and Henry IV was on the
    throne.

58 Christopher Draper] sheriff 1560, Lord Mayor 1566; master
    of the Ironmongers' eight times; died 1581.

60 Alexander Avenons Maioralty . . . Rebells in the North]
    Avenon sheriff 1561, Lord Mayor 1569; Ironmonger eight times
    master of the company; died 1579. Rebellion in the north in
    1569 was largely a Catholic uprising as hundreds of
    peasants, wearing the red cross of crusaders, occupied
    Durham, and held Catholic services in the cathedral. The
    rebels were dispersed, as Mary Queen of Scots was removed to
    a safer place and the Duke of Norfolk was discredited.

61-62 1581, Sir Francis Harvey . . . the French Mounsiers
    comming] [James] Hervey, sheriff 1573, Lord Mayor
    1581; Ironmonger and master of the company four times; his
    son Sebastian Harvey became Lord Mayor in 1618. The
    Frenchman is the Duke of Anjou, who in 1581 made a trip to
    England in behalf of his marriage suit for Elizabeth. He
    was royally entertained, such as in the Whitehall pageant
    participated in by Philip Sidney and others, but went away
    empty-handed.

64 1609, Sir Thomas Cambel] was actually mayor of London in
    1609 though the text reads 1607; Ironmonger and twice master

of the company; sheriff 1600 and 1601; was honoured by
Munday's Lord Mayor's Show of 1609.

69 James Cambel] born 1571; Alderman of Billingsgate;
    sheriff 1619, Mayor 1629, honoured by Dekker's Lord Mayor's
    Show of that year; died January 1642.

83 Peacocks; the second [Pallas] by her Owles; the third
    [Venus] by her Swans] a common emblematic
    representation, also discussed by Heywood in his Gunaikeion,
    p. 8. The ultimate source for Heywood may be Ovid's
    Metamorphoses.

111 Impt] to imp (engraft) wings on or to a person (OED
    cites the pageant text).

132-166 Sagitarius . . . Minerva] much of this material is
    discussed by Heywood in his Gunaikeion (1624).

172 hiemall] winter (OED).

219 munified] fortified, provided with defenses (OED).

252-256 Sicinnius Dentatus . . . was for his Valour, honoured
    with Twenty five severall Crownes] Solinus writes that
    Lucius Sicinius "excelled in valiantnesse among the
    Romaines, the number of hys titles doo declare. . . . Hee
    being vanquisher in eyght challenges hand to hande, hadde
    five and fortie scarres in the forepart of his bodye, and on
    hys backe part not one" (sig El^v) (Golding translation of
    Julius Solinus Polyhistor (London, 1587)).

281f Without these Metalls] a section obviously in praise of
    the Ironmongers, the guild of the new mayor and sponsors of
    the pageant.

283 Coulter and the Share] coulter, iron blade fixed in front
    of the share (iron blade that cuts the ground) OED.

303 snowes] to strew or cover with or as with snow--OED cites
    Heywood's pageant for the use of this word in this sense.

316 fixions] obsolete forms of fiction (OED).

318 Cibus bis coctus] "Food twice cooked."

342 Eutropius reports, Pyrhus to have said] Eutropius reports
    that as Pyrrhus "understoode the sayd Fabricius to be but a
    very pore man, he profered to geve him the fourthe parte of
    his kingdome, if that he woulde forsake Rome, and come to

hym. But Fabricius refused that hys offer . . ." (Book II of the English breviary (1564) version).

347-348 Pericles, who when one had bitterly rayled on him . . .] this episode is reported in Plutarch's Lives, early in the section on Pericles.

354-355 Trajanus the Emperour, that when Sura Licinius . . .] Sura Licinius presumably consul in 97 A.D. (see Ronald Syme, Tacitus (Oxford: Clarendon, 1958), II, 641f.

356 Insidiated] cf. Heywood's use of this word in his 1633 pageant.

363-364 Xenophon reports Cyrus and Agesolanus, to be of such Philosophical patience] the quality of patience is not singled out by Xenophon in any of his writings where he deals with these two men (the latter is presumably Agesilaus). Many virtues are enumerated, but never patience.

386-387 Phinees zelo Inflammatus Confodit scortatorem] "Phineas, kindled with zeal, stabbed the whoremonger." Heywood is apparently recalling the story in the Old Testament account found in Numbers 25.

424 Antecell] to excell (OED cites Heywood's use of this word in this and in the 1638 pageant text).

452-453 Ars Patris, in filiis etiam, post fata viget] "The father's art, in the sons too, flourishes after his death."

Londini Speculum: or,

Londons Mirror, Exprest in sundry Triumphs,

Pageants, and Showes, at the Initiation of the right

Honorable Richard Fenn, into the Maioralty of the Fa-

mous and farre renowned City LONDON.

All the Charge and Expence of these laborious projects both

by Water and Land, being the sole undertaking of the Right

Worshipful Company of the Habberdashers.

Written by Thomas Heywood.

Imprinted at London by J. Okes dwelling in little St.

Bartholmews. 1637.

Londini Speculum : or,

Londons Mirror, Exprest in sundry *Triumphs*, *Pageants*, and *Showes*, at the Initiation of the right Honorable *Richard Fenn*, into the Mairolty of the Famous and farre renowned City *LONDON*.

All the Charge and Expence of these laborious projects both by Water and Land, being the sole undertaking of the Right Worshipful Company of the *Habberdashers*.

Written by Tho. Heywood.   10

Imprinted at *London* by *I. Okes* dwelling in little St. *Bartholmews*. 1637.

Title page of *Londini Speculum* (1637). Reproduced by permission of the Huntington Library, San Marino, California.

To the Right Honour-
able <u>Richard</u> <u>Fenn</u>, Lord
Maior of this Renowned
<u>Metropolis</u> LONDON.

<u>Right</u> <u>Honorable</u>:
<u>Excuse</u> (I intreate) this my boldnesse, which proceedeth rather
from <u>Custome</u> in others, then <u>Curiosity</u> in my <u>Selfe</u>, in presuming to
prompt your <u>Memory</u> in some things tending to the <u>greatnes</u> of your
high <u>place</u> and <u>Calling</u>; You are now entred into one of the most
famous <u>Maioralties</u> of the <u>Christian</u> <u>World</u>. You are also cald   10
<u>Fathers</u>, <u>Patrons</u> of the <u>Afflicted</u>, and <u>Procurators</u> <u>of</u> <u>the</u> <u>Publicke</u>
<u>good</u>. And whatsoever hath reference to the true consideration of
<u>Justice</u> and <u>Mercy</u>, may be <u>Analogically</u> conferd upon pyous and just
<u>Magistrates</u>.

And for the <u>Antiquity</u> of your yearely <u>Government</u>, I read that the
<u>Athenians</u> elected theirs <u>Annually</u>, and for no longer continuance:
And so of the <u>Carthagians</u>, the <u>Thebans</u>, &c. And the <u>Roman</u> Senate
held, that continued <u>Magistracy</u> was in some respects unprofitable to
the <u>Weale-publicke</u>, against which there was an <u>Act</u> in the Lawes of
the twelve Tables. And it is thus concluded by the Learned, that the   20
Dominion of the <u>greatest</u> <u>Magistrates</u> which are <u>Kings</u> and <u>Princes</u>,
ought to be perpetuall; but of the lesse which be <u>Praetors</u>, <u>Censors</u>,
and the like, only <u>Ambulatory</u> and <u>Annuall</u>. I conclude with that
saying of a wise man, Prime Officers ought to Rule by Good Lawes, and
commendable Example, Judge by <u>Providence</u>, <u>Wisdome</u> and <u>Justice</u>, and
Defend by <u>Prowes</u>, <u>Care</u>, and <u>Vigilancy</u>: These things I can but
Dictate, of which your <u>Lordship</u> knoweth best how to Dispose: ever
(as now) remayning your Honors

Humble servant,

<u>Thomas</u> <u>Heywood</u>.   30

Londini Speculum,
or,
Londons Mirrour.

All Triumphs have their Titles, and so this, according to the
nature thereof, beareth a name: It is called Londini κατοπτρον,
that is, Speculum, more plainly, Londons Mirrour, neither altogether
unproperly so termed, since she in her selfe may not onely
perspicuously behold her owne vertues, but all forraigne Cities by
her, how to correct their vices.

Her antiquity she deriveth from Brute, lineally discended from   40
AEneas, the sonne of Anchises and Venus, and by him erected, about
the yeare of the world two thousand eight hundred fifty five: before
the Nativity of our blessed Saviour, one thousand one hundred and
eight: first cald by him Trinovantum, or Troy-novant, New Troy, to
continue the remembrance of the old, and after, in the processe of
time Caier Lud, that is, Luds Towne, of King Lud, who not onely
greatly repaired the City, but increased it with goodly and gorgeous
buildings; in the West part whereof, he built a strong gate, which
hee called after his owne name Lud gate, and so from Luds Towne, by
contraction of the word and dialect used in those times, it came   50
since to be called London.

I will not insist to speake of the name of Maior, which implyeth
as much as the greater, or more prime person; such were the Praetors,
or Proefecti in Rome, neither were the Dictators any more, till
Julius Caesar aiming at the Imperiall Purple, was not content with
that annuall honour, which was to passe successively from one to
another, but he caused himselfe to be Elected Perpetuus Dictator,
which was in effect no lesse than Emperor.

And for the name of Elder-man, or Alder-man, it is so ancient,
that learned Master Cambden in his Britannia remembreth unto us, that 60
in the daies of Royal King Edgar, a noble Earle, and of the Royall
blood, whose name was Alwin, was in such favour with the King, that
he was stiled Healf Kunning, or halfe King, and had the stile of
Alderman of all England: This man was the first founder of a famous
Monastery in the Isle of Ely, where his body lies interred, upon
whose Tombe was an inscription in Latin, which I have, verbatim, thus
turned into English, Here resteth Alwin, couzen to King Edgar,
Alderman of all England, and of this Holy Abbey the miraculous
founder. And so much (being tide to a briefe discourse) may serve
for the Antiquity of London, and the Titles for Maior or Alderman.   70

I come now to the Speculum, or Mirrour. Plutarch tels us, That a
glasse in which a man or woman behold their faces, is of no
estimation or value (though the frame thereof be never so richly
deckt with gold and gemmes, unlesse it represent unto us the true

figure and object. Moreoever, that such are foolish and flattering glasses, which make a sad face to looke pleasant, or a merry countenance melancholy: but a perfect and a true Christall, without any falsity or flattery, rendreth every object its true forme, and proper figure, distinguishing a smile from a wrincle; and such are the meanes many times to bridle our refractory affections: for who being in a violent rage, would be pleased that his servant should bring him a glasse wherein hee might behold the torvity and strange alteration of his countenance? Minerva playing upon a Pipe, was mockt by a Satyre in these words.

80

Non te decet forma istaec, pone fistulas
    Et Arma capesse componens recte genus.
That visage mis-becomes, thy Pipe
    Cast from thee, Warlike dame,
Take unto thee thy wonted Armes,
    And keepe thy Cheekes in frame.

90

But though she despised his Councell for the present, when after, playing upon the same Pipe, in which she so much delighted, shee beheld in a river such a change in her face, shee cast it from her, and broke it asunder, as knowing that the sweetnes of her musick could not countervaile or recompence that deformity which it put upon her countenance, and therefore I have purposed so true and exact a Mirrour, that in it may be discovered as well that which beautifies the governour, as deformes the government.

One thing more is necessitously to be added, and then I fall upon the showes in present agitation: namely, that the fellowship of the Merchant Adventurers of England were first trusted with the sole venting of the manufacture of Cloth out of this kingdome, and have for above this 4 hundred years traded in a priviledged, and wel governed course, in Germany, the Low Countries, &c. and have been the chiefe meanes to raise the manufacture of all wollen commodities to that height in which it now existeth, which is the most famous staple of the Land, and whereby the poore in all Countries are plentifully maintained: and of this Company his Lordship is free: as also of the Levant, or Turkey, and of the East India Company, whose trading hath beene, and is in these forraine adventures: also who spent many yeares and a great part of his youth abroad in other Countries.

100

110

Now the first show by water is presented by St. Katherine, of whom I will give you this short Character: She was the daughter of King Costus, and had the generall title of Queene of Famogosta, because crowned in that City being lineally discended from the Roman Emperors, who as she lived a Virgin so she dyed a Martyr, under the Tyrant Maxentius, whose Empresse with divers other eminent persons she had before converted to the Faith: she rideth on a Scallop,

94

which is part of his Lordships Coate of Armes, drawne in a Sea-
Chariot, by two Sea-horses with divers other adornments to beautifie   120
the peece; the Art of which, the eye may better discover, than my pen
describe, and why she being a Princesse, and Patronesse of this
Company of the Haberdashers, who onely ruled on the Land, should at
this time appeare upon the water, and without any just taxation, to
make that cleare, shee thus delivereth her selfe.

St. Katherines Speech by Water.

    Great Praetor, and grave Senators, she craves
A free admittance on these curled waves,
Who doth from long antiquity professe
Herselfe to be your gratious Patronesse: 130
Oft have I on a passant Lyon sate,
And through your populous streets beene borne in state:
Oft have I grac't your Triumphes on the shore,
But on the Waters was not seene before.

    Will you the reason know why it doth fall,
That I thus change my Element? you shall:
When Triton with his pearly trumpets blew
A streperous blast, to summon all the crew
Of Marine gods and goddesses to appeare,
(As the annuall custome is) and meet you here: 140
As they were then in councell to debate,
What honour they might adde unto the state
Of this Inauguration; there appear'd
God Mercury, who would from Jove be heard:
His Caducaeus silence might command;
Whilst all attentive were to understand
The tenor of his message: who thus spake.

    The Sire of gods, with what you undertake
Is highly pleas'd, and greatly doth commend
That faire designe and purpose you intend;   150
But he beheld a Machine from an high,
Which at first daz'd his immortall eye;
A royall Arke, whose bright and glorious beams
Rivall the Sunnes, ready to proove your streames:
A vessell of such beauty, burthen, state,
That all the high Powers were amaz'd thereat;
So beautified, so munified, so clad,
As might an eight to the seaven wonders adde:
Which must be now your charge; 'twas Joves owne motion,
That all of you attend her to the Ocean.   160

This notwithstanding, such was their great care,
(To shew that o're you they indulgent are)
That Neptune from his Chariot bad me chuse
Two of his best Sea-horses, to excuse
His inforc't absence: Thames (whose breast doth swell
Still with that glorious burthen) bad me tell,
That Joves command shall be no sooner done,
But every Tide he'le on your errands runne
From hence to the Lands end, and thence againe
Backe, to conveigh your trafficke from the Maine:
My message thus delivered; now proceed
To take your oath, there is no further need
Of my assistance; who on Land will meete you,
And with the state of greater Triumphes greete you.

These few following Lines may, (and not impertinently) be added
unto Jupiters message, delivered by Mercury, which though too long
for the Bardge, may perhaps not shew lame in the booke, as being
lesse troublesome to the Reader than the Rower.

Dance in thy raine-bow colours Protaeus, change
Thy selfe to thousand figures, 'tis not strange
With thee, thou old Sea-prophet, throng the seas
With Phorcus Daughters, the Nereides,
And all the blew-hair'd Nymphes, in number more,
Than Barkes that float, or Pibbles on the shore:
Take AEolus along to fill her sailes
With prosperous windes, and keepe within his gailes
Tempestuous gusts: which was no sooner said,
But done: for all the Marine gods obey'd.

The second show, but the first by Land, is presented by the great
Philosopher Pythagoras, Samius, the sonne of Menarchus; which being
outwardly Sphericall and Orbicular, yet being opened it quadrates it
selfe just into so many Angles as there be Scepters, over which his
Sacred Majesty beareth title: namely, England, Scotland, France, and
Ireland, concerning which number of foure, I thus Read: Pythagoras
and his Schollers, who taught in his schooles, that Ten was the
nature and soule of all number; one Reason which he gave (to omit the
rest) was, because all nations, as well civill as barbarous, can tell
no farther than to the Denary, which is Ten, and then returne in
their account unto the Monady, that is one: For example, from Tenne
wee proceed to Eleven and Twelve, which is no more than Ten and One,
Ten and Two, and so of the rest, till the number rise to an infinite.

Againe hee affirmeth, that the strength and vertue of all number
consisteth in the quarternion; for being with the one, two, three and

foure, put them together and they make ten; he saith further, that
the nature of number consisteth in ten, and the faculty of number is
comprized in foure: in which respect the Pythagoreans expresse their
holy oath in the quaternion, which they cal'd τετρακτύν as may
appear in these words.

> Per tibi nostrae animae praebentem tetrada Iuro,
> Naturae fontemque & firmamenta perennis.   210

For they held the soule of man to subsist in that number,
proportionating it into these foure Faculties, Mens, Scientia,
Opinio, Sensus, the Mind, Knowledge, Opinion, and Sence, and
therefore according to that number Pythagoras frames his Speech,
alluding to those foure Kingdomes over which his Majesty beareth
title.

The Speech of the second Show, delivered in
Paules Church-yard.

Sacred's the number foure, Philosophers say,
And beares an happy Omen; as this day   220
It may appeare: foure Elements conspire,
Namely, the Water, Earth, the Aire, and Fire,
To make up man: the colours in him bred
Are also foure, White, Pallid, Blacke, and Red:
Of foure Complexions he existeth soly,
Flegmaticke, Sanguine, Choler, Melancholy.
His meate foure severall digestions gaines,
In Stomacke, Liver, Members, and the Veines.
Foure qualities cald primae within lie,
Which are thus titled, Hot, Cold, Moist, and Drie.   230
He acts his whole life on this earthy stage,
In Child-hood, Youth, Man-hood, Decripit age.
The very day that doth afford him light,
Is Morning the Meridian, Evening, Night.
Foure seasons still successively appeare,
Which put together make a compleat yeare.
The earth, with all the Kingdomes therein guided,
Is into foure distinguish'd parts devided.
The foure Windes from the World foure quarters blow,
Eurus, Favonius, Auster, Aquilo.   240
All Morall vertues we in foure include,
As Prudence, Justice, Temperance, Fortitude.
Court, City, Campe, and Countrey, the foure C's,
Which represent to us the foure degrees,

Requir'd in every faire and flourishing Land,
Substract but one a Kingdome cannot stand.
Foure Colonels are in this City knowne,
Of which you, honoured Sir, have long beene one:
And those foure Crownes (for so the high Powers please)
Embleme the Kings foure Scepters, and foure Seas.   250
The fift Imperiall Arch above, proclaimes   Quinta per-
That glorious Crowne, at which his Highnesse aimes.   ennis.
Thus is our round Globe squard, figuring his power,
And yours beneath Him, in the number foure.

The third Show.

    The third Pageant or Show meerly consisteth of Anticke
gesticulations, dances, and other Mimicke postures, devised onely for
the vulgar, who are better delighted with that which pleaseth the
eye, than contenteth the eare, in which we imitate Custome, which
alwaies carrieth with it excuse: neither are they altogether to be   260
vilefied by the most supercilious, and censorious, especially in such
a confluence, where all Degrees, Ages, and Sexes are assembled, every
of them looking to bee presented with some fancy or other, according
to their expectations and humours: Since grave and wise men have
beene of opinion, that it is convenient, nay necessitous, upon the
like occasions, to mixe seria iocis; for what better can set off
matter, than when it is interlaced with mirth?   From that I proceede
to the fourth.

The fourth Show.

    It beareth the Title of an Imperiall Fort: nor is it compulsive,   270
that here I should argue what a Fort is, a Skonce, or a Cittadall,
nor what a Counterskarfe, or halfe Moone, &c. is; nor what the
opposures or defences are: my purpose is onely to expresse my selfe
thus farre, that this Fort which is stil'd Imperiall, defenc'd with
men and officers, suiting their functions and places proper to such a
muniment, doth in the morall include his Majesties royall chamber,
which is the City of London, for to that onely purpose was the
project intended.

    The Speaker is Bellona, whom some held to be the Daughter, some
the Sister, others the Nurse of Mars the god of Warre; neither in any   280
of these is any impropiety, or ought that is dissonant from
authority, because Enyo, which is Bellona, implyeth that which
putteth spirit and courage into an army, &c. Antiquity called her

98

Duellona, that is, the goddesse of warre, to whom their Priests
sacrificed their owne blood, and before whose Temple the Faecialis
set a speare against some prime pillar thereof, when any publicke
warre was to be denounced: Shee was most honoured of the Thracians,
the Scithians, and those wild and barbarous nations, upon whose
Altars they used to sacrifice a Vulture, which is a ravenous bird,
used to prey upon dead carcasses, and assemble themselves in great   290
flocks after any fought battaile: but this Discourse may to some
appeare impertinent to the project in hand, and therefore I thus
proceed to her speech.

Bellonaes Speech upon the Imperiall Fort.

      This Structure (honour'd Sir) doth title beare
Of an Imperiall Fort, apt for that spheare
In which you now moove, borrowing all her grace,
As well from your owne person, as your place;
For you have past through all degrees that tended
Unto that height which you have now ascended.   300

      You have beene in this City ('tis knowne well)
A Souldier, Captaine, and a Colonell.
And now in times faire progresse, to crowne all,
Of this Metropolis chiefe Generall.
You, of this Embleme, which this day we bring,
To represent the Chamber of the King,
Are the prime governour: a Royall Fort,
And strongly scited, as not built for sport,
But for example and defence: a Tower
Supported by no lesse than Soveraigne power: 310
The Theologicke vertues, the three Graces,
And Charites have here their severall places.
Here Piety, true Zeale, study of Peace,
(By which small mites to Magozines increase)   Concordia
Have residence: now opposite there are   parve res
To these, and with them at continuall warre,   Crescunt,
Pride, Arrogance, Sloath, Vanity, Prestigion,   is the Mot-
Prophanesse, the contempt of true Religion,   to of the
With thousands more, who assiduatly waite,   Company
This your Imperiall Fort to insidiate.   of the
                                                                                  right Wor-
      You may observe i'th' musicke of your Bels   shipfull
Like sound in Triumphes, and for funerall knels;   Habber-
Marriage and death to them appeare all one,   dashers.
Masking nor mourning cannot change their tone:
With our Fort 'tis not so, whose faire pretence, is
To comply with the nature of offences,

<u>Errors</u>: she knowes in low termes how to chide
<u>Great</u> faults, with greater noise are terrifi'd:
But she can load her Cannons, and speake loud
To encounter with the arrogant and proud: 330
Whats further in your <u>Praetorship</u> assign'd,
You, in your <u>Londons</u> <u>Mirrour</u> there may find.

<u>The</u> <u>fifth</u> <u>show</u>, <u>cald</u> Londons Mirrour.

This beareth the title of the whole Triumphe; of Glasses
pertinent to this our purpose, there bee severall sorts, as <u>Opticke</u>,
<u>Perspective</u>, <u>Prospective</u>, <u>Multiplying</u>, &c. The presenter is <u>Visus</u>,
or Sight; for what the minde is to the soule, the same is the eye to
the body, being the most precious part thereof. Sight is the most
soveraigne sence, the first of five, which directeth man to the
studdy and search of knowledge and wisedome; the eyes are placed in 340
the head as in a Citadel, to be watch towers and Centinels for the
safety, and guiders and conducters for the sollace of the body.

We reade that one <u>Marcus</u> <u>Varro</u> was sir-named <u>Strabo</u>, for the
excellency and quicknesse of his sight, who from <u>Libaeum</u>, a Province
in <u>Scicilia</u>, could distinguish and give an exact account of all such
ships as came out of the haven of <u>Carthage</u>, which two places some
hold to be more than an hundred <u>Italian</u> leagues distant: indeed no
man can better estimate the vertue and value of the sight, than he
that is made blinde and wants it, neither could I devise a more apt
Speaker to present this <u>Mirrour</u>, than the sence of the sight, without 350
which, the purest Christall is of no use at all.

The Pageant it selfe is decored with glasses of all sorts: the
persons upon or about it are beautifull Children, every one of them
expressing their natures and conditions in the impresaes of their
shields, eight of the prime of which suiting with the quality of the
<u>Optick</u> sence, beare these severall Inscriptions: <u>Aspice</u>, <u>Despice</u>,
<u>Conspice</u>, <u>Prospice</u>, <u>Perspice</u>, <u>Inspice</u>, <u>Circumspice</u>, <u>Respice</u>:

᾽Ὄψις, or <u>Opsis</u> the Speaker.

Behold me <u>Sight</u>, of the five sences prime, 360
(Now best complying with the place and time)
Presenting <u>Londons</u> <u>Mirrour</u>, and this Glasse
Shewes not alone what she is, or once was,
But that the spacious Universe might see
In her, what their great Cities ought to be;

That every forraigne Magistrate from hence
Might learne how to dispose his Opticke sence.

    Aspice saith, Looke toward and upon
Desartfull men whom this Age frowneth on.
And Despice cast downe thy powerfull eye
On the poore wretch that doth beneath thee lye.   370
Then Conspice take counsell first and pause
With meditation, ere thou judge a cause.
Prospice bids looke a farre off, and view
(Before conclude) what dangers may insue.
Perspice wils, in sifting doubts, then scan
The nature of the matter with the man.
Let every cause be searcht, and duely sought,
Saith Inspice, ere thou determinst ought.
Circumspice saith, looke about to immure
So great a charge, that all within be sure.   380
Considerate Respice injoynes thee last,
To cast thine eyes backe upon all things past.

    For Londons selfe, if they shall first begin
To examine her without, and then within,
What Architectures, Palaces, what Bowers,
What Citadels, what turrets, and what towers?
Who in her age grew pregnant, brought a bed
Of a New Towne, and late delivered
Of such a burthen, as in few yeares space,
Can almost speake all tongues, (to her more grace.)   390
Then her Cathedrals, Temples new reparing,
An act of true devotion, no man sparing
His helping hand; and many, 'tis well knowne,
To further Gods house have forgot their owne.

    Unto her outward shape I doe not prize her,
But let them come within to anatomize her.
Her Praetor, scarlet Senate, Liveries,
The ordering of her brave societies:
Divine Astraea here in equall scale
Doth ballance Justice, Truth needes not looke pale,   400
Nor poverty dejected, th' Orphants cause,
And Widowes plea finde helpe; no subtile clause
Can make demurre in sentence: a faire hearing,
And upright doome in every Court appearing:
    Still to preserve her so, be't your indeavour,
    And she in you, you her shall live for ever.

    I come now to the Linvoy, or last Speech, when his Lordship,
after his dayes long and tedious trouble, retireth himselfe to his
rest at night, in which Pythagoras the Speaker briefly runs over the
passages of the Pageants before expressed after this manner.   410

The Speech at Night.

We to a Valediction are confin'd,
(Right Honoured) and intreat You beare in minde
What was this Day presented: Your chiefe Saint
A Martyr once of the Church militant,
But now of the tryumphant, bids You spare
Your selfe this Night: for to a World of Care
You are ingag'd to morrow, which must last
Till the whole progresse of Your Yeere be past.
The Spheare-like Globe quadrated, lets You know,   420
What Pro-Rex doth to the foure Scepters owe.
Your Military honours, (in your Dayes
Of lesse command) th' Imperiall Fort displayes,
And Londons Mirrour, that all men may see
What Magistrates have beene, and ought to be.
Set is the Sunne long since, and now the Light
Quite fayling us, Thrice Honourd Sir, good Night.

   For the Artists, and directors of these Pageants and showes, John
Christmas and Mathias, the two Sonnes of Gerard, their now deceased
Father, a knowne Master in all those Sciences he profest: I can say   430
no more but thus, that proportioning their Workes according to the
limits of the gates through which they were to passe, being ty'de not
to exceede one Inch either in height, or breadth: My opinion is,
that few Workemen about the Towne can paralell them, much lesse
exceede them. But if any shall either out of Curiosity or malice
taxe their ability, in this kind of Art, I referre them to the
Carving of his Majesties Great Ship lately built at Woolwitch, which
Worke alone is able both to satisfie Emulation, and qualifie Envie.

FINIS.

Textual Notes

Heywood's <u>Londini Speculum</u> (Greg, <u>Bibliography</u>, no. 552; STC
13349) survives in six copies, found in the Bodleian Library, Library
of St. John's College (Oxford), Chapin Library, Huntington Library,
and the Guidhall Library (2 copies). The press variants, which all
occur on the inner forme of sheet C, are recorded in the Collation
below. All copies have been collated. This pageant text also
appears in the 1874 Heywood edition, volume 4, and it has been
collated also and significant changes recorded.

One of the interesting things about the printing of this quarto
is the change in the size of type font that occurs on sig. C4^v.
Obviously the compositor miscalulated in casting off copy; the change
to a smaller font prevents the pamphlet from running onto another
sheet. A similar change can be seen in another Heywood text printed
by John Okes earlier in 1637. In <u>A</u> <u>True</u> <u>Description</u> <u>of</u> <u>His</u> <u>Majesties</u>
<u>Royall</u> <u>Ship</u>, printed probably in September 1637, the compositor
changes to a smaller font on sig. G3 in order to complete the text on
G4^v; thus he is able to get thirty-two prose lines per page, whereas
he had been averaging about twenty-six.

The only uncorrected copy of <u>Londini Speculum</u> is one of the
Guildhall Library copies, which I have arbitrarily designated copy
#2. Overall, the printing of <u>Londoni Speculum</u> is unusually clean;
only in sheet C did some errors slip through.

Collation

(title page) Maioralty] Mairolty Q, 1974

 10 <u>Maioralties</u>] <u>Mairolties</u> Q, 1874

 45 remembrance] remembrancer 1874

 60 in his] 1874; in in his Q

 63 he] 1874; be Q

242 Temperance,] Temperance Q, 1874

243 C's] CCCs Q, 1874

251 (margin) Quinta perennis] Bodleian, Oxford, Chapin,
     Huntington, Guildhall #1 (1874); Quinta paennis Guildhall
     #2

267 when] all copies except one (1874); mhen Guildhall #2

271 Cittadall] all copies except one (1874); Cittudall
Guildhall #2

321 th'] th Q, 1874

354 impresaes] all copies except one (1874); impressures
Guildhall #2

Commentary Notes

Sir Richard Fenn, Haberdasher, was inaugurated with the usual
ceremonies, and once again Heywood prepared a pageant for this guild.
Though the guild records show evidence of establishing committees to
arrange the pageant, there are no examples of payments to Heywood or
anyone else.

2 Richard Fenn] sheriff 1626, Lord Mayor 1637; died 1638 or
1639; son of Hugh Fenn of Wotton.

40-51 Brute] cf. Heywood's earlier poem Troia Britanica and
Anthony Munday's 1605 Lord Mayor's Show, The Triumphs of Re-
United Britiannia, where a very complete treatment of the
story is given dramatic life in a civic pageant.

60 Master Cambden in his Britannia] William Camden's Britannia
(London, 1586); English translation 1610.

71 Plutarch tels us] a close approximation to this statement
cited by Heywood is found in Plutarch's Moralia, "How to
tell a Flatterer," in which he uses the image of the mirror
(vol. I, p. 285 of the Loeb edition).

82 torvity] fierce look, grimness (OED's earliest examples
are 1639 and 1650).

98 deformes] forms, fashions (Obs. rare--OED).

112f St. Katherine] cf. the discussion of Katherine in
Heywood's Gunaikeion (1624), p. 374, and of course the
discussion and appearance of this saint in Heywood's 1631
and 1632 pageants.

131 on a passant Lyon sate] as Catherine did in the 1632
pageant. The lion forms part of the heraldic crest of the
Haberdashers.

175-178 These few . . . Rower] a rare instance in which the pageant dramatist calls attention to something included in the text that did not occur in the performance itself.

206-207 <u>Pythagoreans</u> expresse their holy oath in the <u>quaternion</u>] on p. 58 of Heywood's <u>Gunaikeion</u> there is a discussion of the Pythagoreans and the number four as well as the oath.

209-210 <u>Per tibi</u> . . . <u>perennis</u>] This odd phrase seems to mean: "I sweare to you through (the one) offering the tetrad to our soul, the source and firmament of perennial nature." Heywood may have taken his idea from Martianus Capella, Book VII "Of Arithmetic" in <u>The Marriage of Philosophy and Mercury</u>, item #734.

271 Skonce] a small fort or earthwork (OED).

272 Counterskarfe] (counterscarp) outer wall or slope of the ditch which supports a covered way (OED).

317 Prestigion] a delusion, trick, illusion (Obs. rare). OED cites this 1637 pageant text.

343-344 <u>Strabo</u>, for the excellency and quicknesse of his sight] As Solinus records: "The quickest of sight was one <u>Strabo</u>, whom <u>Varro</u> avoucheth to have overlooked a hundred thirty & five miles, and that hee was wont exactlie to viewe from the watch Towre of <u>Lyliby</u> in <u>Sicill</u>, the Punicke fleete setting out of the Haven of <u>Carthage</u>, and to reporte the just number of their Shipper" (sig E1^v).

428-429 <u>John Christmas</u> and <u>Mathias</u>] this is the second of the pageants for which these sons of Gerard Christmas serve as the artificers, their father having died in 1634.

436-437 I referre them to the Carving of his Majesties <u>Great Ship</u>] more details of this ship are provided in Heywood's own pamphlet on the subject, <u>A True Description of His Majesties Royall Ship</u> (London, 1637); on p. 47 Heywood mentions the work of the Christmas brothers.

Porta Pietatis,

or,

The Port or Harbour of Piety.

Exprest in sundry Triumphes, Pageants,

and Showes, at the Initiation of the

Right Honourable Sir MAURICE ABBOT

Knight, into the Maioralty of the famous

and farre renowned City London.

All the charge and expence of the laborious Projects

both by water and Land, being the sole undertaking

of the Right Worshipfull Company of

the Drapers.

Written by Thomas Heywood.

Redeunt Spectacula

Printed at London by J. Okes. 1638.

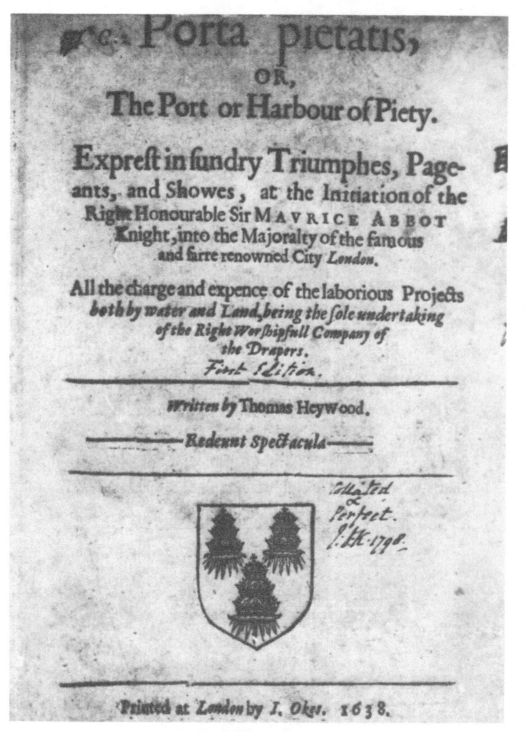

Porta Pietatis,

OR,

The Port or Harbour of Piety.

Exprest in sundry Triumphes, Pageants, and Showes, at the Initiation of the Right Honourable Sir MAVRICE ABBOT Knight, into the Majoralty of the famous and farre renowned City *London.*

All the charge and expence of the laborious Projects *both by water and Land, being the sole undertaking of the Right Worshipfull Company of the Drapers.*

First Edition.

Written by Thomas Heywood.

───── *Redeunt Spectacula* ─────

Collated & Perfect. I.H. 1798.

Printed at *London* by I. *Okes.* 1638.

Title page of *Porta Pietatis* (1638). Reproduced by permission of the Huntington Library, San Marino, California.

To the Right Honorable Sir Maurice
Abbot, Knight, the Lord Maior of this
renowned Metropolis, London.

Right Honourable:
Antiquity informes us, in the most flourishing state of Rome, of
an Order of the Candidati, so called, because habited in white
vesture, betokning Innocence, and those of the noblest Citizens, who
in that garbe walked the streets with humble lookes, and submisse
gesture, thereby to insinuate themselves into the grace of the
people, being ambitious after honour and Office. Great Lord, it
fareth not so with You, who though for inward Candor and sincerity,
You may compare with the best of them, yet have beene so far from
affecting such popularity, that though You in Your great Modesty
would willingly have evaded it; yet some places by importunity, and
this Your present Praetorship hath by a generall suffrage, and the
unanimous harmony of a free Election, beene conferd upon You.

Neither can I omit the happinesse of Your deceased Father,
remarkable in three most fortunate Sonnes: the one, for many yeares
together, Arch-Bishop of Canterbury, and Metropolitane of all
England: another, a reverend Father in God, Bishop of Salisbury: as
memorable for his learned Workes and Writings, as the other for his
Episcopall government in the Church, and Counsell in state. And now
lately Your Honour'd selfe, the Lord Maior of this Metropolis, the
famous City London: In which, and of which, as you are now Maximus,
so it is expected you shall prove Optimus. Grave Sir, it is a knowne
Maxime, that the honour which is acquired by Vertue, hath a
perpetuall assurance: nor blame my boldnesse, if I presume to prompt
Your memory in what You have long studied: The life of a Magistrate
is the rule and square whereby inferior persons frame their carriage
and deportment, who sooner assimulate themselves to their Lives than
their Lawes, which Lawes if not executed are of no estimation. But I
cease further to trouble Your Lordship, leaving you to Your
Honourable charge, with that of the Poet,

Qui sua metitur pondera, ferre potest.

Your Lordships in all observance

Thomas Heywood.

10

20

30

Londini Porta
Pietatis:
Londons Gate to Piety.

London and Westminster are two Twin-sister-Cities; as joyned by
one Street, so watered by one streame: the first a breeder of grave
Magistrates, the second, the buriall-place of great Monarchs; Both
famous for their two Cathedrals: the one Dedicated to the honour of
Saint Paul, the other of Saint Peter. These I rather concatenate,
because as in the one, the Right Honourable the Lord Maior receiveth
his honour, so in the other he takes his Oath: yet London may be
presum'd to be the elder, and more excellent in Birth, Meanes, and
Issue; in the first for her Antiquity, in the second for her Ability,
in the third, for her numerous Progeny: she and her Suburbs being
decored with two severall Burses or Exchanges, and beautified with
two eminent Gardens of Exercise, knowne by the names of Artillery and
Military. I shall not need to insist much either upon her Extension,
or Dimension, nor to compare her with other eminent Cities that were,
or are, it having beene an Argument treated of by Authentick Authors,
and the laborious project of many learned Pennes, and frequently
celebrated upon the like dayes of Solemnity.

And although by the space of Tenne yeares last past, there hath
not beene any Lord Maior free of that Company, yet was there within
Twelve yeeres before that six Lord Maiors of the same. And it shall
not bee amisse to give you a briefe Nomination of some Honourable
Praetors, and those of prime Remarke in that Company: Sir Henry
Fitz-Alwin Draper, was the first Lord Maior of this Citie, which
place hee held for foure and twenty yeeres together, and upward; and
in the first yeere of his Maioralty, Anno 1210, London-Bridge, which
was before made of Timber, was begun to be built of Stone. Sir
William Powltney was foure times Lord Maior; 1337 he built a Chappell
in Pauls, where hee lyeth buried, and erected a Colledge neere unto
the Church of St. Laurence Powltney, London: He moreover built the
Church of little Alhallows in Thames street, with other pious and
devout Acts. John Hind Draper, Lord Maior 1405, built the Church of
St. Swithen by London-stone, &c. Sir John Norman was the first that
rowed in his Bardge to Westminster, when hee went to take his Oath:
Sir Richard Hardell sate in the Judicatory Seate six yeares
together: Simon Eyre Lord Maior, built Leaden-Hall at his owne
proper costs and charges: Sir Richard Pipe, George Monox, Lord
Maior 1515, and Sir John Milborne, were great Erectors of Almes-
houses, Hospitalls, &c. and left liberally to the poore: Sir Richard
Campion perfected divers charitable workes, left unfinish't by Sir
John Milborne before named. Sir Thomas Hayes 1615, Sir John Jolls
1616, Sir Edward Barkham, Sir Martin Lumley, Sir Allan Cotten, Sir
Cuthbert Hacket, &c. To speake of them all, I should but spend Paper
in a meere capitulation of their names, and neglect the project now
in agitation.

The first Show by Water.

    The first Show by Water is presented by Proteus in a beautiful
Sea-Chariot: for the better Ornament, decored with divers Marine
Nymphs and Sea-goddesses, &c. He sitteth or rideth upon a moving
Tortois, which is reckoned amongst the Amphibiae, quod in ambobus
Elementis degant: That is, One of those Creatures that live in two
Elements, the Water, and the Land; alluding to the Trading of the   90
Right Honourable the present Lord Maior, who is a Merchant, free of
the Turkey, Italian, French, Spanish, Muscovy, and was late Governour
of the East Indy-Company. This Proteus, or πρῶτος that is Primus,
is held to be the first, or most ancient of the Sea-gods, the Sonne
of Oceanus and Thetis, who could transhape himselfe into any Figure
whatsoever, and was skilfull in Prediction: He was call'd Vertumnus
ὰ vertendo, because he indented or turned the course of the River
Tyber, which floweth up to Rome, as the Thames to London; he was a
King, and reigned in the Carpathian Island, which because it was full
of boggs and marish places, (as lying neere unto the maine Ocean) he   100
had that Title conferr'd on him to be a Marine god: when the
Scithians thought to invade him, and by reason of the former
impediments could no way damage his Countrey, it therefore increased
their superstitious opinion to have him Deified. He was called also
Pastor Populi, that is, A Shepheard of the people; and is said also
to feede Neptunes Fishes call'd Phocae.

    It was a Custome amongst the AEgyptian Kings, to have their
Scepters insculpt with sundry Hierogliphicks, or Figures, as a Lyon,
a Dragon, a Tree, a flame of fire, &c. as their fancies lead them,
for which that Proverb has conferr'd on him, Proteo mutabilior, that   110
is, More changeable than Proteus. This Proteus, or Vertumnus, or
Vesores, reigned in AEgypt some foure yeeres before the Trojan Warre,
that is, Anno Mundi, 2752.

Proteus his Speech.

    Proteus of all the Marine gods the prime,
And held the noblest both for Birth and Time:
From him who with his Trident swayes the Maine,
And ploughs the waves in curles, or makes them plaine:
Neptune, both Lord of Ebbe, and Inundation,
I come to greete your great Inauguration.   120
They call me Versi-pellis, and 'tis true,
No figure, forme, no shape to me is new;
For I appeare what Creature I desire,
Sometimes a Bull, a Serpent, sometimes Fire:
The first denotes my strength; strong must he be,
And powerfull, who aspire to your Degree.

110

You must be wise as Serpents, to decide
Such doubts as Errour or Misprision hide.
And next, like Fire, (of th' Elements most pure)
Whose nature can no sordid stuffe endure,   130
As in Calcining Metalls we behold,
It sunders and divides the drosse from Gold,
And such are the Decorements that still waite
Upon so grave, so great a Magistrate.

      This Tortois, double-natur'd, doth imply
(By the two Elements of moist and dry)
So much as gives the world to understand,
Your noble Trading both by Sea and Land.
Of Porposes the vast Heards Proteus keepes,
And I am styl'd the Prophet of the Deepes,   140
Sent to praedict good Omen: May that Fleete
Which makes th' East Indies with our England meete,
Prosper to all your hearts desires: Their sayles
Be to and fro swell'd with auspicious gales:
May You (who of this City now take charge)
With all the Scarlet Senate in your Barge,
The Fame thereof so heighten, future Story
Above all other States may crowne her glory.
      To hinder what's more weighty, I am loath,
      Passe therefore freely on, to take your Oath.   150

      This Show is after brought off from the water to attend upon the
rest by Land, of which the first is,

                    The first Show by Land.

      A Shepheard with his Skrip and Bottle, and his Dog by him; a
sheep-hooke in his hand, round about him are his Flocke, some
feeding, others resting in severall postures; the plat-forme adorn'd
with Flowers, Plants, and Trees bearing sundry Fruits. And because
this Worshipfull Society tradeth in Cloth, it is pertinent that I
should speake something of the Sheepe, who is of all other foure-
footed beasts the most harmelesse and gentle. Those that write of   160
them, report, that in Arabia they have tayles three Cubits in length:
In Chios they are the smallest, but their Milke and Cheese the
sweetest, and best. The Lambe from her yeaning knoweth and
acknowledgeth her Damme: Those are held to be most profitable for
store, whose bodies are biggest, the fleece softest and thickest, and
their legs shortest. Their Age is reckoned at Tenne yeeres, they
breed at Two, and cease at Nine: The Ewes goe with their young an
Hundred and fifty dayes. Pliny saith, the best Wooll Apulia and
Italy yeelds, and next them Milesium, Tarentum, Canusium, and
Laodicea in Asia; their generall time of sheering is in July: The   170

Poet <u>Laberius</u> called the Rammes of the Flocke <u>Reciproci-cornes</u>, and
<u>Lanicutes</u>, alluding to the writhing of their Hornes and their Skinnes
bearing <u>Wooll</u>: The Bell-weather, or Captaine of the Flocke is call'd
<u>Vervex</u> <u>sectarius</u>, &c.

The <u>Shepheards</u> Speech.

By what rare frame, or in what curious Verse
Can the rich profits of your Trades commerce
Be to the full exprest? which to explaine,
Lyes not in <u>Poets</u> Pen, or <u>Artists</u> braine.
What Beast, or <u>Bird</u>, for Hyde, or Feather rare,   180
For mans use made, can with the <u>Sheepe</u> compare?
The <u>Horse</u> of strength or swiftnesse may be proud,
But yet his flesh is not for food allow'd.
The <u>Heards</u> yeeld Milke and Meate (commodious both)
Yet none of all their skins make <u>Wooll</u> for <u>Cloth</u>.
The <u>Sheepe</u> doth all: The <u>Parrot</u> and the <u>Jay</u>,
The <u>Peacock</u>, <u>Estridge</u>, all in colours gay,
Delight the Eye, some with their Notes, the Eare,
But what are these unto the <u>Cloth</u> we weare?

Search Forrests, Desarts for Beasts wilde or tame,   190
The Mountaines or the Vales, search the vast frame
Of the wide <u>Universe</u>, the Earth, and Skie,
Nor Beast nor <u>Bird</u> can with the <u>Sheepe</u> comply:
No Creature under Heaven, bee't small or great,
But some way <u>usefull</u>, one affords us <u>meate</u>,
Another <u>Ornament</u>: Shee more than this,
Of <u>Patience</u>, and of <u>Profit</u> th' <u>embleme</u> is,
In former Ages by the <u>Heroes</u> sought:
After, from <u>Greece</u> into <u>Hesperia</u> brought:
She's cloath'd in plenteous riches, and being shorne,   200
Her <u>Fleece</u> an <u>Order</u>, and by <u>Emperours</u> worne,
All these are knowne, yet further understand,
In twelve divide the profits of this Land,
As Hydes, Tinne, Lead; or what else you can name,
Tenne of those twelve the Fleece may justly claime:
Then how can that amongst the rest be mist,
By which all States, all Common Weales subsist?
    Great honour then belongs unto this trade,
    And you, great Lord, for whom this triumph's made.

The <u>second</u> <u>Show</u> <u>by</u> <u>Land</u>.   210

The second Show by land is an <u>Indian</u> Beast, called a <u>Rinoceros</u>,
which being presented to the life, is for the rarenesse thereof, more
fit to beautifie a Triumph: his Head, Necke, Backe, Buttockes,
Sides, and Thighes, armed by Nature with impenetrable Skales; his
Hide or Skinne of the colour of the Boxe-tree, in greatnesse equall
with the Elephant, but his Legges are somewhat shorter: an enemy to
all beasts of rapine and prey, as the Lyon, Leopard, Beare, Wolfe,
Tiger, and the like: but to others, as the Horse, Asse, Oxe, Sheep,
&c. which feede not upon the life and blood of the weaker, but of the
grasse and hearbage of the field, harmlesse and gentle, ready to   220
succour them, when they be any way distressed. Hee hath a short
horne growing from his nose, and being in continuall enmity with the
Elephant, before hee encounter him, he sharpeneth it against a stone,
and in the fight aimeth to wound him in the belly, being the softest
place about him, and the soonest pierc'd: He is back't by an <u>Indian</u>,
the speaker.

The <u>Indians</u> Speech.

   The dignity of Merchants who can tell?
Or how much they all Traders ante-cell?
When others here at home securely sleepe,   230
He plowes the bosome of each unknowne deepe,
And in them sees heavens wonders; for he can
Take a full view of the <u>Leviathan</u>,
Whose strength all Marine Monsters doth surpasse,
His Ribs as Iron, his Fins and skales as brasse.

   His ship like to the feather'd Fowle he wings,
And from all Coasts hee rich materialls brings,
For ornament or profit; those by which
Inferiour Arts subsist, and become rich:
By Land he makes discovery of all Nations,   240
Their Manners, and their Countries scituations,
And with those savage natures so complies,
That there's no rarity from thence can rise
But he makes frequent with us, and yet these
Not without dangers, both on shores and seas:
This Land he pierceth, and the Ocean skowers,
To make them all by free transportage ours.

   You (honourd Sir) amongst the chiefe are nam'd,
By whose commerce our Nation hath beene fam'd.
The <u>Romans</u> in their triumphes had before   250
Their Chariots borne or lead, (to grace the more
The sumptuous Show) the prime and choisest things,
Which they had taken from the Captive, Kings:
What curious Statue, what strange bird, or beast

That Clime did yeeld (if rare above the rest)
Was there expos'd: Entring your civill state,
Whom better may we strive to imitate?

This huge Rinoceros (not 'mongst us seene,
Yet frequent where some Factors oft have beene)
Is embleme of the Praetorship you beare,
Who to all Beasts of prey, who rend and teare
The innocent heards and flocks, is foe profest,
But in all just defences armes his crest.
You of this wildernesse are Lord, so sway,
The weake may be upheld, the proud obey.

260

The third Show by Land.

The third Show by land is a Ship, fully accommodated with all her
Masts, Sayles, Cordage, Tacklings, Cables, Anchors, Ordnance, &c. in
that small Modell, figuring the greatest Vessell: But concerning
Ships and Navigation, with the honour and benefits thence accrewing,
I have lately delivered my selfe so amply in a Booke published the
last Summer of his Majesties great Shippe, called the Soveraigne of
the Seas, that to any, who desire to be better certified concerning
such things, I referre them to that Tractate, from whence they may
receive full and plenteous satisfaction: I come now to a yong Sailor
the Speaker.

270

The Speech from the Shippe.

Shipping to our first Fathers was not knowne;
(Though now amongst all Nations common growne)
Nor trade by Sea: we read the first choise peece,
Was th' Argo, built to fetch the golden Fleece,
In which brave voyage, sixty Princes, all
Heroes, such as we Semones call:
In that new Vessell to attaine the shore.
Where such a prize was, each tugg'd at the Oare:
On one bench Hercules and Hilas sate,
Beauty and Strength; and siding just with that
Daunaus and Lynceus of so quicke a sight
No interposer, or large distance might
Dull his cleare Opticks: those that had the charge,
And the chiefe stearadge of that Princely Barge,
Zethes and Calais, whose judgements meet,
Being said t' have feathers on their heads and feete:
We spare the rest: Grave Sir, the Merchants trade

280

290

Is that, for which all Shipping first was made:
And through an Hellespont who would but pull,
Steere, and hoise-saile, to bring home golden Wooll?
For wee by that are cloath'd: In the first place
Sate strength and beauty: oh what a sweete grace
Have those united; both now yours, great Lord,   300
Your beauty is your robe, your strength the sword.

　　You must have Lynceus eyes, and further see
Than either you before have done, or he
Could ever: having now a true inspection
Into each strife, each cause without affection
To this or that party: some are sed,
To have had feathers on their feete and head.
(As those whom I late nam'd) you must have more,
And in your place be feather'd now all o're:
You must have feathers in your thoughts, your eyes,   310
Your hands, your feete; for he that's truely wise
Must still be of a winged apprehension
As well for execution, as prevention.
You know (Right honourd Sir) delayes and pauses,
In judicature, dull, if not dampe, good causes:
　　That we presume t' advise, we pardon crave,
　　It being confest, all these, and more you have.

The fourth Show by Land.

　　The fourth Show by Land beares the Title Porta Pietatis, The Gate
of Piety: which is the doore by which all zealous and devout men   320
enter into the fruition of their long hoped for happinesse: It is a
delicate and artificiall composed structure, built Temple-fashion, as
most genuine and proper to the persons therein presented. The
Speaker is Piety her selfe, her habit, best suiting with her
condition; upon her head are certaine beames or raies of gold,
intimating a glory belonging to sanctity; in one hand an Angelicall
staffe, with a Banner; on the other Arme a Crosse Gules in a field
Argent: upon one hand sits a beautifull Childe, representing
Religion, upon whose Shield are figured Time, with his daughter
Truth: her Motto Vincit veritas: In another compartment sitteth one 330
representing the blessed Virgin, Patronesse of this Right Worshipfull
Society, Crowned: in one hand a Fanne of Starres, in the other a
Shield, in which are inscribed three Crownes (gradatim) ascending,
being the Armes or Escutchion of the Company, and her Motto that
which belongeth unto it: Deo soli Honor & gloria: that is, unto God
onely be Honour and Glory: Next her sit the three Theologicall
Graces, Faith, Hope, and Charity, with three Escutchions, Faiths
motto, Fidei ala, Caeli scala: The wings of Faith are the ladder by
which we scale heaven. Hopes, Solum spernit qui Caelum sperat: hee

hates the Earth, that hopes for Heaven. Loves Motto, <u>Ubi charitas</u>, 340
<u>non est Caritas</u>, <u>who giveth willingly</u>, <u>shall never want wretchedly</u>.
A sixth personateth <u>Zeale</u>, in whose Escutchion is a burning Hart:
Her word; <u>In tepida</u>, <u>frigida</u>, <u>flagrans</u>: neither <u>luke-warme</u>, <u>nor key-</u>
<u>cold</u>, <u>but ever burning</u>: A seventh figureth <u>Humility</u>: Hers, <u>In terra</u>
<u>Corpus</u>, <u>in Caelo Cor</u>: the body on earth, the heart in Heaven. And
last <u>Constancies</u>: <u>Metam tangenti Corona</u>; <u>A Crowne belongeth to him</u>
<u>who persevereth to the end</u>. I come to the Speech.

<u>Piety</u> the Speaker.

This Structure is a Citadell, or Tower,
Where <u>Piety</u>, plac't in her heavenly bower, 350
Poynts out the way to blisse, guirt with a ring
Of all those Graces that may glory bring.
Here sits <u>Religion</u> firme, (though else where torne
By Schismaticks, and made the Atheists scorne)
Shining in her pure truth, nor need she quake,
Affrighted with the Faggot and the stake:
Shee's to you deare, you unto her are tender,
Under the Scepter of the Faiths defender.

How am I extasi'de when I behold
You build new Temples, and repaire the old! 360
There's not a stone that's laid in such foundation,
But is a step degreeing to Salvation:
And not a Scaffold rear'd to that intent,
But mounts a Soule above the Firmament:
Of <u>Merchants</u>, we know <u>Magistrates</u> are made,
And they (of those) most happy that so Trade.

Your <u>Virgin-Saint</u> sits next <u>Religion</u> crown'd
With her owne Hand-maids (see) inviron'd round,
And these are they the learned Schoole-men call,
The three prime Vertues Theologicall, 370
<u>Faith</u>, <u>Hope</u>, and <u>Love</u>; <u>Zeale</u> all inflam'd with fire
Of devout acts, doth a sixt place aspire.
The seventh <u>Humility</u>, and we commend
The Eight to <u>Constancy</u>, which crownes the end.

A Triple Crowne's th' Emblazon of your Crest,
But to gaine one, is to be ever blest.
Proceede in that faire course you have begun,
So when your Annuall Glasse of State is run,
(Nay, that of Life) <u>Ours</u>, but the <u>Gate</u> to blisse
Shall let you in to yon <u>Metropolis</u>. 380

116

There now remaineth onely the last Speech at Night, spoken by
Proteus, which concludes the Tryumph.

The Speech at Night.

Now bright Hiperion hath unloos'd his Teame,
And washt his Coach-Steeds in cold Isters streame:
Day doth to Night give place, yet e're You sleepe,
Remember what the Prophet of the Deepe,
Proteus fore-told: All such as State aspire,
Must be as Bulls, as Serpents, and like Fire.
The Shepheard grazing of his Flocks, displayes   390
The use and profit from the Fleece we raise.
That Indian Beast, (had he a tongue to speake)
Would say, Suppresse the proud, support the weake.
That Ship the Merchants honour loudly tells,
And how all other Trades it antecells:
But Piety doth point You to that Starre,
By which good Merchants steere: too bold we are
To keepe you from your rest; To-morrows Sunne
Will raise You to new cares, not yet begun.

I will not speake much concerning the two Brothers, Mr. John and   400
Mathias Christmas, the Modellers and Composers of those severall
Peeces this day presented to a mighty confluence, (being the two
succeeding Sonnes of that most ingenious Artist Mr. Gerard Christmas)
to whom, and to whose Workmanship I will onely conferre that
Character, which being long since (upon the like occasion) conferr'd
upon the Father, I cannot but now meritedly bestow upon the Sonnes:
Men, as they are excellent in their Art, so they are faithfull in
their performance.

FINIS.

Textual Notes

Porta Pietatis, Heywood's 1638 Lord Mayor's Show (Greg, Bibliography, no. 546; STC 13359) is extant in seven copies, found in the Huntington, Guildhall, Harvard University, Society of Antiquaries (imperfect copy; lacks title page and dedication), Bodleian, British Library, and the National Library of Scotland. The press variants, recorded below, suggest perhaps more than one round of correction; the variants occur in each sheet of the quarto. An edition of Porta Pietatis appears in F. W. Fairholt's Lord Mayors' Pageants, part 2 (London: Percy Society, 1844), pp. 61-78. The text in the 1874 edition of Heywood, volume 5, largely follows the Fairholt 1844 edition. These editions have been checked against the quarto copies, all of which have been collated.

Collation

(title page) Maioralty] Majoralty Q, 1874

  7 betokning] betokening 1874

45 Maior] 1874; Major Q

58 Maior] Major Q, 1874

59 yeeres] years 1874

59 Maiors] Majors Q, 1874

62 Maior] Major Q, 1874

64 Maioralty] Majoralty Q, 1874

66 Maior] Major Q, 1874

70 Maior] Major Q, 1874

74 Maior] Major Q, 1874

76 Maior] Major Q, 1874

91 Maior] Major Q, 1874

110 conferr'd on] Society of Antiquaries (1847); conferr'd in all other copies

115 Marine] main 1874

125   The first] 1874; "The first Q (ll. 125-132 all begin
      with quotation marks)

197   Of Patience] 1874; "Of Patience Q

201   Her Fleece] 1874; "Her Fleece Q

212   is for] Huntington, British Library, Society of
      Antiquaries, Guildhall, Bodleian (1874); more for Harvard,
      National Library Scotland

309   feather'd now] Huntington, British Library, Society of
      Antiquaries, Guildhall, Bodleian (1874); feather'd new
      Harvard, National Library Scotland

330   compartment] copartment Q, 1874

344   Hers,] Her's Q; her's: 1874

380   to yon] Huntington, British Library, Society of
      Antiquaries, Guildhall, National Library Scotland (1874); to
      you Harvard, Bodleian

392   had] hae 1874

393   Would] Woule 1874

395   Trades] Traees 1874

Commentary Notes

For the Drapers, Heywood wrote this pageant honoring Sir Maurice
Abbot, the new mayor. A total of £747. 2s. was spent on the show.
Guild records spell out the agreement with the Christmas brothers and
Heywood: "Item paid to John Christmas and Matthew Christmas by
agreement for making and setting out of five Pageants or showes as by
the printed booke they are particularly described and for all charges
incident to those shewes and also to find Greene men and ffireworkes
and to discharge Mr Thomas Hayward the Poet for writing the booke and
furnishing the Company with 500 bookes the some of Clxx^{11} and of the
Companies well liking it, x^{11}" (Collections, p. 127). Thus the
Christmas brothers received a basic payment of £180, a fairly
standard payment.

1-2   Maurice Abbot] [Morris] sherrif 1627; Alderman
      Bridge Without; MP Hull 1620-22 and later for London; died
      1642.

8   submisse] submissive

19 Arch-Bishop of Canterbury] this brother of Maurice Abbot
    is George Abbot (1562-1633) who became Archbishop in 1611.

20 Bishop of Salisbury] Robert Abbot (1560-1618) elder
    brother of George and brother of Maurice; in 1615 he became
    Bishop of Salisbury, consecrated by his brother, the
    Archbishop of Canterbury.

26-27 Maxime . . . assurance] perhaps a variation of the
    proverb, "Honour is the reward of virtue."

33-34 Qui sua metitur pondera, ferre potest] "He who
    measures his burdens can bear them."

44 concatenate] to connect together (see 1631 pageant).

50 Burses or Exchanges] the Royal Exchange built by Thomas
    Gresham and the New Exchange (1609) in the Strand.

51-52 Artillery and Military] the original Artillery Garden
    in London is now marked by Artillery Lane and Artillery
    Street, Bishopsgate Street Without; later, in 1641, the
    practice area was moved to Finsbury. Stow describes the use
    of the Artillery Garden in his Survay of London (1618), p.
    320. Essentially this was a practice field for the
    Fraternity of Artillery, joined by wealthy citizens and
    country gentlemen. The Military Garden is Leicester Fields
    or Square in the parish of St Martin's-in-the-Fields; this
    was also a brick, walled "garden" for artillery exercise.
    For further information, consult Henry B. Wheatley, London
    Past and Present (London: Murray, 1891), vols. 1 and 2.

61-62 Henry Fitz-Alwin] first Lord Mayor of London; see 1631
    show.

66 William Powltney] Heywood has confused this person with
    the man who was actually Lord Mayor, John de Pulteney; mayor
    in 1333; Alderman for Coleman Street.

70 John Hind] [Hend] mayor 1405; refounder of St.
    Swithin's church, London stone.

71 John Norman] mayor 1453; son of William Norman of
    Banbury, Oxfordshire; MP 1448 and 1449.

73 Richard Hardell] (1253-1258), served as sheriff with John
    Tolason in 1249.

74 Simon Eyre] founder of Leadenhall, and a donor in
    addition of 5000 marks for relief of the poor; the subject
    of Dekker's play, The Shoemaker's Holiday; mayor 1445.

75 Richard Pipe] mayor 1578; son to Richard Pipe of
Wolverhampton.

75 George Monox] [Monnoux] mayor 1514; re-edified the
decayed parish church of Walthamstow, Essex; founded a free-
school and almshouses there.

76 John Milborne] mayor 1521; founder of the almshouses at
Crutched friars.

77-78 Richard Campion] [Champion] mayor 1565; increased
Milborne's charity at Crutched friars.

79 Thomas Hayes] sheriff 1604; mayor 1614; born about 1548;
Alderman of Bishopsgate and of Cornhill; died in 1617.
Honored in Munday's 1614 Lord Mayor's Show, Himatia-Poleos.

79 John Jolls] son of Thomas Jolles of Stratford-le-Bow; was
Alderman of Tower 1605 until his death in 1621; sheriff
1605; mayor 1615; honored by Munday's Lord Mayor's Show of
1615, Metropolis Coronata.

80 Edward Barkham] mayor 1621; sheriff 1611; honored by
Middleton's mayoral pageant of 1621; admitted of Gray's Inn
1608; Alderman of Farringdon Within and of Cheapside; died
1634.

80 Martin Lumley] son of James Lumley; born about 1580;
sheriff 1615; mayor 1623, honored by Middleton's show;
Alderman of Vintry and of Broad Street; President of
Christ's Hospital, 1632-34; died 1634.

80 Allan Cotten] mayor 1625; son to Ralph Cotton of
Whitchurch.

81 Cuthbert Hacket] mayor 1626; son of Thomas Aket or Hacket
and grandson of Thomas Aket or Hacket of Dartford, Kent;
honored by Lord Mayor's Show of 1626, written by Thomas
Middleton.

161 in Arabia . . . length] this detail Heywood may have
picked up from Topsell, p. 599.

162 Chios] Greek Aegean island. Edward Topsell writes: "the
sheepe of the Isle Chius, are very small, and yet their
Milke maketh very lawdable cheese" (p. 598, Four-footed
Beastes).

168-69 Pliny saith . . . yeelds] Natural History, Book VIII,
lxxiii, "The most highly esteemed wool is the Apulian and
the kind that is called in Italy wool of the Greek breed and

elsewhere Italian wool. The third place is held by the
sheep of Miletus. . . . they [Apulian fleeces] have a
very high reputation in the districts of Taranto and
Canossa, as have the Laodicean fleeces of the same breed in
Asia."

171 Poet Laberius] (c. 115-43 B.C.) together with Pubililus
Syrus elevated to literary standards the popular southern
Italian mimus (mime). Aulus Gellius accuses him of
extravagance in coining new words.

211f a Rinoceros] for information about the rhinoceros,
consult Edward Topsell's The History of Four-footed Beastes
and Serpents (London, 1607), pp. 594-97. Tospell draws the
contrast with the elephant.

229 ante-cell] to excel (OED cites and the earlier use in
the 1635 pageant). See below l. 395.

271-272 Booke published . . . great Shippe] see the note for
the 1637 pageant concerning the "Great Ship."

302 Lynceus eyes] Lynceus, son of Aphareus and Arene, and
brother of Idas, one of the Argonauts, and famous for his
keen sight. Cooper's Thesaurus (London, 1565) includes
reference to him, claiming that he could see 130 miles;
"they that have verye sharpe syghtes, be sayde to have
Lynceos oculos, the eyes of Lynceus" (sig. L3^v).

331 blessed Virgin] striking and unusual is this
representation of the Virgin in mayoralty pageants, her
presence justified by her being patron of the Drapers.

333 three Crownes] a reference to the arms of the Drapers.
The triple crown is a direct allusion to the Virgin, to whom
the guild from its earliest days had been devoted.

343-344 neither luke-warme, nor key-cold] Biblical allusion,
see Revelation 3:15-16.

Londini Status Pacatus:

or,

LONDONS Peaceable Estate.

Exprest in sundry Triumphs, Pageants, and
Shewes, at the Innitiation of the right Honourable
HENRY GARWAY, into the Maioralty of the Fa-
mous and farre Renowned City LONDON.

All the Charge and Expence, of the laborious
Projects both by Water and Land, being the sole un-
dertakings of the Right Worshipfull Society of Drapers.

Written by THOMAS HEYWOOD.

Redeunt Spectacula

Printed at London, by John Okes. 1639.

Londini Status Pacatus :

OR,

LONDONS Peaceable Estate.

Exprest in sundry Triumphs, Pageants, and
Shewes, at the Innitiation of the right Honourable
HENRY GARVVAY, into the Majoralty of the Fa-
mous and farre Renowned City LONDON.

All the Charge and Expence, of the laborious
Projects both by Water and Land, being the sole un-
dertakings of the Right Worshipfull Society of *Drapers*.

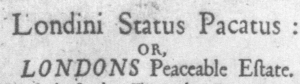

Written by THOMAS HEYVVOOD.

Redeunt spectacula

Printed at *London*, by *Iohn Okes*. 1639.

Title page of *Londini Status Pacatus* (1639). Reproduced by permission of the
Huntington Library, San Marino, California.

To the Right Honorable
Henry Garway, Lord Maior of
this Famous Metropolis, London.

Right Honourable,
To whom for your long Travell, variety of Language, and knowne
Wisedome, I cannot but give a precedence due to your Person, as a
priority belonging to your place; since laboured lines onely comply
with judicious eares. I must ingeniously confesse your worth so
farre to transcend my weakenesse, that I am almost silent in the
Proem ere I enter on the Epitasis: yet presuming on your generous
disposition, which ever waiteth on sollid Judgement, I thus proceede.

Your breeding (Right Honourable) next to a Scholler hath beene
chiefly in Mercature, and of your sufficiency therein, you have not
onely given to this City ample satisfaction; but to the severall
parts of this Christian World: your personall Travell in your youth
acquainting you with the passages and proceedings in other forraigne
regions, have bettered your conceptions (now growing towards Age) in
the management of State Magistracy in your native Realme: of which
since the time that you were first chosen Alderman, you have given
rare President; none having decided more differences, ended more
doubtfull Causes; or beene a greater Peace-maker than your honoured
selfe.

And for the multiplicity of your Commerce, it is most manifest,
that you have long Traded (to begin with the nearest first) in the
Low Countries, France, Spaine, Italy, Venice, East India; and
moreover in Greene-land, Muscovy, and Turkey, of which three noble
societies last named you are at this present Governour. History
tells us that divers Praetors and Tribunes during the time of their
Authority, have bin so indulgent over the people committed to their
charge; that they have not onely ratified the good Edicts of others,
but devised wholsome Ordinances of themselves: when Solon swayed the
Senate no Creditor had power over the Debters bodies, but their goods
onely. In Platoes Common-weale all excesse was prohibited, which
amongst the Romans was cald Lex sumptuaria. Acilius glabrio made an
Edict De pecuniis repitundis, Commanding all mony taken by bribery,
extortion, or other indirect meanes to bee restored, cald Lex Acilia:
Another compelled the Plebe to a liberall contribution towards all
publicke Showes, and Triumphs; which was Titled Lex fannia.

But not to indanger the just reproofe of a presumptious
arrogance, in prompting your Lordships in the studied Duties of your
succeeding charge, I conclude with that Spanish Refran: Embia al
sabio a la embaxada, Y no le degat nada; still remembring that of
Cato, Imperium gero non mihi sed Civitati et sociis.

Your Honours most obsequious

Thomas Heywood.

126

Londini Status
Pacatus: or
Londons Peaceable Estate.

Not to insist upon the Antiquity, Nobility, nor the first
foundation and scituation of this glorious City, comparing it with   50
others (of old) rarely remarkable; now demolisht and ruin'd: neither
with those contemporary or at this present in greatest prosperity,
either for Magnificent structure, or Grave and godly Government;
because it hath bin the Annuall argument, suiting with the occasion
now in agitation: let them therefore passe as conclusions granted,
and principles against which there is no disputation to be held;
since for beautifull Architectures, Pallaces, Rialtoes, Guilds,
Arcenalls, Temples, Cathedralls, Aquaeducts &c. and further for
commerce in al Countries, Christian or Heathen, discoveries,
plantations, (as in Ireland, Virginia, Bromoothos, or Summers   60
Islands, St Christophers, New England, Harber-grace in New-found Land
&c.) In which the most famous Cities of the World, Athens, Thebes,
Lacedemon, nor Rome it selfe the Metropolis of the Roman Empire,
could in her most flourishing estate and Potency, (though she
Tyranniz'd over the whole World,) in the least compare with London.
And in the way of Competitor-ship, the Spartan Ephori, the Athenian
Areopagitae, with Romes purple Optimates, may subscribe to her
scarlet Senate; no Pretor in any City whatsoever being graced with
the like Sollemne and sumptuous Inauguration.

But from the City, I come now to the particular Company of the   70
Drapers, one of the prime members thereof; which may claime one
speciall priority above the rest: in regard that Sir Henry Fitz-
Alwin was of that Fraternity, and the first Lord Maior, who might bee
rather cald a perpetuall Dictator than an one yeares Praetor;
continuing his Maioralty from foure and twenty yeares and upwards
together: not Anno completo, but vita durante; from his Initiation,
to his Expiration: which hath not hapned in any other of the eleven
Worshipfull Societies. After him within a little space, Sir William
Powltney foure yeares together Lord Maior, John Hind, Sir John New-
man, Sir Richard Hardell, before whom the Sword was borne for the   80
space of sixe severall yeares without intermission. Simon Eyre who
built Leaden Hall, or Sir Richard Pipe, George Monox, Sir John
Milborne, Sir Richard Campion, Sir Thomas Hayes, Sir John Jolls, Sir
Edward Barkham, Sir Martin Lumley, Sir Allen Cotten, Sir Cutbert
Hacket, and Sir Maurice Abbot, whom the Right Honourable Henry Garway
now succeedeth: the right Worshipfull Mr. Thomas Adam, being this
yeare Sheriffe, and of the Drapers Society.

And although before the last Lord Maior preceeding this, there
hath not bin any for the space of ten yeares of that Worshipfull
fraternity, yet in the Annuall vicessitude of twelve yeares before,   90
sixe of those before named were elected into the Praetorian dignity:
and all, or most of these from the first being builders of Churches,
and Chappels; Founders of Schooles, Almes-houses, and Hospitalls,

repayrers of decayed Temples, and Oratories; Benefactors to Halls, and liberall contributors to the maintaining of Arts, and all Pious and Charitable acts whatsoever. Besides your Coate of Armes, Nobilitated by ancient Heraldry, being three imperiall Crownes supported by two golden pelletted Lions; your Crest Aries, the first of twelve Zodiack signes; your inscript, To God alone be all honour and glory: your Patronesse, the blessed Virgin; all these approve   100
your antiquity and dignity: I have nominated these amongst many, &c. but I come now to the first shew by water.

The first Shew by water.

Is a person representing the ancient River Nilus, mounted in a Sea-Chariot, and seated upon a silver Scallop (the plat-forme decored with Marine Nimphs and Goddesses) his habit suiting with the nature of the river, in his right hand a seven-forked Scepter, alluding to the seven heads, or as many Channells through which he runnes; and therefore by Ovid, cald Septem-fluus: he is drawne by two Crocadiles, which may be reckoned amongst the Amphibiae, as living   110
in, and pertaking of the two Elements, Earth and Water: the river it selfe by sundry Inundations watereth the whole Land of AEgypt, leaving behind it a slime, or moist Clay, which serveth for a marle or manuring, to make the soyle more fertill. The originall head from which it flowes is uncertaine, which Claudian thus expresseth: Et Arcanos Nili deprendite fontes. The Ecclesiasticall Writers hold it for one of the foure rivers that floweth from the earthly Paradise; in divers places it changeth name, according to the scituation of the shores through which it runnes: it brings forth Reedes, whose filmes or inward rinds are much like our Paper, and for a need may be writ   120
upon; and therefore by the Poets cald Nilus papyrifer: of all other rivers it onely breedeth Crocadiles, and Hippotami, AEqui fluviales, Sea Horses.

The Crocadile is a Serpent that from a small Egge, growes in short time to a mighty length and bignesse, for some of them have bin 22 Cubits long; it hath four feet, with which he runnes as swiftly on land as hee swims by water; he is bold over those that fly him, but fearefull of those that pursue him; the foure winter moneths, November, December, January, and February, he eats not at all; hee hath no tongue, but teeth sharpe and long; neither in feeding doth he   130
move his lower jaw: briefly, hee is terrible to man and beast, and preyes on both; but I leave them and come to the speaker.

128

Nilus.

Nilus an ancient River, knowne to excell
Amongst those foure, (which before Adam fell
Watred the earthly Paradise) now claimes
A new alliance with his brother Thames.

Martia, so cald of Marsius, who to win
The praise from great Apollo, lost his skin:
Amphrisus, who his name shall ever keepe,   140
Since there Apollo kept Admetus Sheepe.
Nor yet Cremera, by whose firtile side
Three hundred and six Fabii at once dide.
Xantus, and Simois, those too famous floods,
So often stain'd in Greeke and Trojan bloods:
Nor let Pharsalian Enepeus boast
In Caesars triumph, o're great Pompies hoast:
Deucalion bragge not of Cephisus for'd,
Because neere it lost man-kind he restor'd:
Caister of her Swans, Permessus cleere,   150
Proud that the Muses were delighted there.
Pactolus, nor Idaspes, fam'd of old
For glittering Channells, pav'd with pearle and gold,
Let none of these compare with aged Nile,
Who onely breeds the weeping Crocodile:
Who drew me hither to the Celebration,
Of this your great loud voyc'd inauguration.

Grave and judicious Praetor, O make me
Your Happy Embleame; since as I foresee
By reason, that in AEgypt falls no raine,
There needs must be a dearth of grasse and graine;   160
Therefore, by frequent Inundations, I
In my great care, that needfull want supply:
So Magistrates (of which you prime and best
We must acknowledge) ought to the distrest:
In your known gravity and goodnesse cast
The future to provide for, salve what's past.

My seven-fold Scepters Hierogliphick, tels
Seven heads, from which (my mighty river swels),
Seven liberall arts (by you maintaind) expresse
Your Cities magnitude and worthinesse.   170

And as you see my Crocodiles I sway,
(Monsters, which both by land and water prey)
If any such here breed? as some no doubt,
In place and Office may be; search them out:
And then, what greater honour can you claime,
Then such rude beasts like me to curbe and tame?
But y' are too long detain'd; I next commend you,

Unto those Triumphs that on Land attend you.

The second Shew, but the first by Land

Is Janus, plac'd upon an Artificiall Structure, built in a square   180
modell, at the foure corners whereof sit foure Persons representing
the foure seasons; Spring, Summer, Autume, Winter; every one habited
agreeable to his propriety and condition. The name Janus is borrowed
from the Hebrew word Iain, which implyeth Vinum, wine, being held to
bee the first that planted the Vine. Some report him to have bin an
ancient King of Italy amongst the Aborigines, Anno Mundi 2629, and
before Christ 1319, who received Saturne flying from his Son Juptier,
and taught him the use of Agriculture and Tillage. Historians report
him to have bin the wisest King in his dayes; remembring things past,
and predicting what was futurely to come; and therefore they figured   190
him with two faces: he was Deified after his death, to whom Numa
dedicated a Temple, shut in the time of peace, open in the time of
warre; from which he had the denomination of Janus Patuleius, and
Clausius: some thinke him to have bin Ogyges, others Noah, with one
face looking backward upon the world before the Flood, the other
forward on that since the Flood: they also called the one the face
of Government, the other of Labour. His standing upon such fixt
bases admonisheth all Magistrates, and men of Honour, to be constant
in all their courses; but especially in the establishing and
maintenance of true Religion: He holdeth in his right hand a golden   200
Key to shut up the yeare past, as never more to come, and open to the
yeare future: it may also be an Embleme of noble policy to unbosome
and bring to light their trecherous devises and stratagems, who seeke
to undermine and supplant the prosperity of a faire and flourishing
Common-weale. Upon the Key are two Greeke letters ingraven, ξ and
ε and on a bar in his left hand the letter τ all being numerall,
and make up 365, the number of the dayes in our solary yeare; of
which by some hee is stil'd the Father: the bar in his left hand
implyeth the Fortitude required in every good Magistrate, in the
incouragement of vertue, and suppressing of vice &c. Janus the   210
speaker:

His speech as followeth.

I Janus, the yeares Father, in my prime
Almost as soone as either light, or time;
Hither my servants the foure Seasons bring
Cold Winter, Autumne, Summer, and the Spring.
Eleven Moneths are my Sonnes, my Daughter May
Makes up the twelft: her Sisters Night, and Day
Acknowledge me their Father: Girles of spleene

130

So oppos'd, they never will at once bee seene.
The Houres my Hand-maids are, which imploy'd well,   220
Shall make you in your Praetor-ship excell
(As all the rest fore-nam'd): Behold this Key,
With which I ope the gates of Land and Sea
To the time future; being made by me
To all your Trade, commerce, and Trafficke free.
Proceede and prosper, whilst the yeare fore-past
(As never more to come) I shut up fast;
One face still looking backe, least good Acts done
Might be obscur'd in darke oblivion:
As th' other forward, to see what's to doe;   230
Both for Gods Honour, and your Countryes to.

    From Janus this use may it please you gather,
You for one yeare are made the Cities Father;
These foure succeeding Seasons, I resigne
Unto your charge; (which I before cald mine):
To the twelve Moneths, most aptly may comply
Your twelve chiefe Companies: who can deny
My Daughter Day for your imployment prest?
The blacke-brow'd Night, sequestred for your rest?
So spend the Houres to inrich future story,   240
Both for your owne grace and the Cities glory.

    My golden Key make use off, to set wide
Those Prison gates, where many a soule hath dide,
Starv'd by th' Oppressors cruelty; those Gaild
For Capitall crimes, unpittied, and unbaild,
Reserve for publicke Triall: Justice is bound
To cut of Gangreenes, to preserve the sound:
But none knowes better than your selfe (Grave Lord)
What Mercy is; or when to use the Sword.

                    The third Show   250

    Is Orpheus with his Harpe, seated in a faire Plat-forme,
beautified with pleasant Trees, upon which are pearcht severall
Birds, and below Beasts of all sorts, who notwithstanding being of
severall conditions, and opposite natures, yet all imagined to be
attentive to his Musick. This Show hath reference to the title of
the whole Triumph, Status pacatus, A peaceable and blest estate, in
which our Soveraigns Royalty hath a correspondence with Saturnes
Reigne, which was cald the golden world. There were foure most
excellent of the Harpe, remembred unto us by the ancient Poets, who
are likewise the Emblemes of the foure Elements: Apollo the Son of   260
Jupiter and Latona, (killing the Dragon Pithon) of fire. Amphion the
Son of Jupiter an Antiope, figured with a Camelion of Ayre. Arion
the Methimnian riding upon a Dolphin, of water: and Orpheus the

Thracian (thus accomodated) of the Earth: and these attributes were
confer'd on them for their severall Ayres, and straines in Musick:
this Orpheus was the Sonne of Apollo, who instructed him on the
Harpe, upon which he grew so excellent that the Woods and Mountaines
followed him; the Rivers staid their course, and the wild beasts, and
birds their prey, with Trees, and stones were said to be attentive to
his Musick: of him much more might be spoken, but to shorten   270
circumstance I come to his Speech.

                              Orpheus.

        Inquire from all antiquity, 'tis said
That when Apolloes Son, (I Orpheus) plaid
Upon my Harpe, the rivers if they swel'd
Above their bankes or Torrents that rebeld,
Grew smooth to heare my musicke: and forbore
To vexe the Channels, or molest the Shore.
The Panther, Tyger, the wild Boare, the Beare,
Forget their rage, to give me attentive eare,   280
Lions with Lambs together coucht in love,
As dreadlesse by the Falcon pearcht the Dove:
The Hounds their pursuite did leave off, and there
Sate Hart, and Hare, close by them without feare:
The sad predicting Raven, from the Oake
(Hollowed with age) was not once heard to croake,
Nor any Bird of harsh throate: onely then
The Nightingale, the Robin, and the Wren
With all their musicall quire, in silent groanes,
(Affraide to sing out) cherrupt to my Tones.   290
The very Trees I did so much intrance,
They shooke their bowes because they could not dance:
But, Stones not rooted, but above the ground
Mov'd in rare postures to my Harps sweet sound:
I the foure blustering Brothers rage make calme,
And 'stead of violent gusts to breath soft balme.

        Yet there's an Harmony which doth rejoyce
Mans heart, more than the Instrument, or Voyce;
The Gitterne, Harpe, the Viol, and the Lute,
When that is heard to sound may all stand mute;   300
Whose happy Symptoms more contentment brings
Than any Consort, made by breath or strings:
And sends a sweeter rapture to the eares
Than that above, made by th' orbicular Spheares.

        May it your grave Pretorian wisedome please,
You are that Orpheus who can doe all these:
If any streame beyond its bounds shall swell,
You beare the Trident that such rage can quell.

When beasts of Rapine (trusting to their power)
Would any of your harmelesse flocks devoure: 310
Yours is the sword that can such violence stay,
To keepe the Rich from rigour, Poore from prey;
Neither from any harsh ill-boading beake,
Least discord shall be heard, when you but speake;
Whilst in Harmonious quire the rest contend,
Which in your praise each other shall transcend.

Trees rooted in selfe-will, and (which seemes strange)
Even sencelesse stones you into life may change,
This Wisedome can; yet there's a more Devine
Concordancy, which farre exceedeth mine: 320
That's of unanimous hearts; plenty, increase;
With all Terrestriall blessings waite on peace:
Which whilst maintain'd in your Commerce and Trade,
Proves sweeter Musicke than e're Orpheus made.

The fourth Show

Is a Chariot drawne by two Cammells, upon eithers back an Indian
mounted, and habited according to the manner of their Country: of
Cammells there be two sorts, the Bactrian, and Arabian; and differ
thus: The Bactrians have two bunches or swellings on the backe, and
are called Dromedaries: the Arabians but one, and another on the   330
breast, on which they leane when they lye downe to rest: They want
the upper order of teeth, and are some times used in War, in velocity
exceeding horses; but most commonly for burdens, every one being
acquainted with his owne lading according to his strength; lesse
weight they desire not, and more they will not beare: they are
taught to kneele till they have their load, and then they rise of
themselves. Neither in their journey will they change their pace;
they can abstaine from water foure dayes together, but then they
drinke as well for the time past, as that to come; yet not before
with their feet they have troubled the streame: they live to fifty   340
yeares, and some to an hundred; and though the pelleted Lyons might
have serv'd more properly to this place, as being supporters of the
Armes belonging to the Right Worshipfull Company of the Drapers; yet
these are as genuine to the purpose: to show his Lord-ships generall
negotiation in all kinds of Merchandise whatsoever.

I cannot stand to speake much of the Fleece, but of Jason, and
Medea, (thus briefly); Jason signifieth sanans, or healing, Medea
consilium, or Counsell: he was the Son of AEson, his Father was no
sooner dead but he left the Kingdome to his brother Pelias, who set
him upon an adventure to fetch the golden Fleece from Colchos: to   350
which purpose hee caused the Argoe to be built, in which sixty of the
prime Princes of Greece accompanied him; whom Medea, the Daughter of
AEtes King of Colchos courteously entertained with all the rest of

the Argonauts: and being greatly inamoured of him, and affraide
least he should perish in the attempt; knowing the danger he was to
undergoe, upon promise of Marriage, she taught him how he should tame
the Brazen-footed Bulls, and to cast the Dragon that watched the
Fleece into a dead sleepe: which hee did, and by slaying him bore
away the prize. The rest I leave to the Speaker which is

Medea.   360

    Thus doth the daughter of the Colchian King,
Her Husband Jason home in Triumph bring,
After his mighty Conquest of the Fleece;
The Aureum vellus brought from thence to Greece.

    And wast not a brave prise? for who so dull
Cannot conceive the worth of golden wooll?
The mornings Sun upon their Fleeces shines,
Making the fields appeare like richest Mines.

    One of the first we reade of was the Ram,
Upon whose back Phrixus and Helle swam   370
The Hellespont: she to her lasting fame
(By being drown'd there, gave the Sea that name):
But Phrixus safely did to Colchos steere,
And on Joves Alter sacrificed there
The golden Beast, whose faithfull service done,
With the Celestiall gods such favour won;
That striving 'mongst themselves to have him grac'd,
Him first of all the Zodiak signes they plac'd.

    And worthily, search the vast earth or deep,
No beast to man, so usefull as the sheep: 380
How many poore men doth it keepe in pay,
Of several Trades and faculties; else they
Might starve for want of lively-hood: but their charge bearing
By Carding, Spinning, Weaving, Fulling, Shearing.
How with her flesh we are satisfi'd within,
Cloath'd with her Wooll without; in whose shorne skin
Those reverent antiquities are kept,
Which else long since had in oblivion slept:
And for the Fleece it selfe, it is an honour;
First Nature, and since Time, hath cast upon her,   390
So great, so eminent, so meriting praise,
Even Emperours were it on their Feastivall dayes:
And none that ever her true vertue knew,
But rated her with Ophir, and Peru.

    These Cammels though amongst us rarely seene,
Yet frequent where your Lordship oft hath beene

134

In your long Travells: may the world perswade
The rich Commerce and noblenesse of your Trade.

    Time so contracts us, that we cannot dwell
On all in which you Merchants most excell: 400
Yet honor'd Sir, what's in this place deny'd
Shall in <u>Pacatus Status</u> bee supply'd.

                        The <u>fifth</u> <u>Show</u>.

    As the last had a relation to the Company in generall, so this
hath reference to his Lordship in particular, as he is a noble
Merchant; having it hereditary from his worthy Father Mr. <u>William</u>
<u>Garway</u>, who was not onely a great Benefactor to the Right Worshipfull
Society of the <u>Drapers</u>, but an indulgent Educator of divers yong men,
who have since prov'd great and Eminent adventurers; some attaining
even to the prime Magistracy of this our Metropolis.   410

    The next Modell presented to the publick view is a Ship, which as
it hath all accomodatings and ornaments belonging to such a Vessell;
so it is also decored with the Armes of the nine Companies of
Merchant-adventurers, of which his Lordship hath bin, and is at this
present free: the trouble of the place, the presse of so mighty a
confluence, with the necessity of time, in the solemnity of such a
Feastivall Day (then limited) will not afford it a speech: which I
the rather omit; because in the last representation of the like, the
excellency of Merchandise, the commodity of shipping, with the
antiquity and profit of Navigation was delivered at large: I   420
therefore come to the sixt and last, which is

    An artificiall Architecture best able (for the Workeman-ship) to
commend it selfe, and being apparent to the publick view, lesse
needeth my description. It presenteth the calamities of War, and the
blessednesse of peace, <u>Status Pacatus</u>; bearing the Title of the whole
Triumph: In one part thereof are exprest to the life, the figures of
<u>Death</u>, <u>Famine</u>, <u>Sicknesse</u>, <u>strage</u>, &c. in the other <u>Prosperity</u>,
<u>Plenty</u>, <u>Health</u>, <u>Wealth</u>, but especially the free and frequent
Preaching of the Word and Gospell. I desire not to swell these few
pages to small purpose, therefore thus briefly of both. Peace is the 430
Tranquility, and calme quiet of Kingdomes, free from Section, tumult,
uproares and faction; a Plantation of rest, ease and security; with
all the flourishing ornaments of earthly felicity: peace is the end
at which War aimeth; Honour the fruits of peace; and good Goverment
the ground of either, asking no lesse wisedome to preserve it, then
valour to obtain it: for Concord and Unity maketh a mite to increase
to a Magazin, when discord and debate in any publick Weale, or
private society, lesseneth a mountaine to a Mole-hill; and therefore
<u>Pacem te poscimus omnes</u>.

Now of the contrary, War is of two sorts, Civill, or Forraigne. 440
Domesticke War is the over-throw and ruine of all Estates, and
Monarchies, and the incendiary of whatsoever is most execrable,
begetting contempt of God, corruption of manners, and disobedience to
Magistrates, change of Lawes, neglect of Justice, and dis-estimation
of Learning and liberall Arts: But forraigne Warre is that (by
Plato, cald a more gentle and generous contention) onely lawfull,
being undertooke to propagate true Religion; or to procure a
continuance of Peace. Any War may be begun with great facility, but
is ended with much difficulty; neither is it in his power to end it
who begins it: to raise a combustion is in the power of any Coward, 450
but to appease it lyes onely in the mercy of the Conquerour: and
therefore much safer and better is certaine peace, than hoped for
Victory: the first is in our Will, the latter in the Will of the
Gods.

      Ergo Fames, pestis, Bellum grassantur in omnes,
         Vivere si vultis, vivite iam melius.
      By War, Plague, Famine, (loe) the people fall;
      Then better live: if you will live at all.

The more to illustrate this Tryumph, it is graced by the Company
of Artillery men compleatly armed, to expresse Warre: and the Livery
and gown-men being the Embleme of Peace. I come now to the Speech, 460
delivered by The Genius of the City.

      War, to the unexperienc'd, pleasant showes,
      But they who in the Progresse and the Close
      Shall trace it, know it horrid; 'Tis a time
      Destin'd, to the revenge, and scourge of Crime:
      A time, when numerous armies, with the stresse
      Of mailed men, and harnest Horses, presse
      Grones from the trembling Earth (with feare astounded)
      And with the reeking gore of slaine and wounded
      Drencht her instead of Raine: when like shooting Comets 470
      Its lightning bolts the thundring Cannon vomets;
      Quaking the bellowing Ayre: when shrill alarmes,
      Rushing of rowted Troopes, clashing of Armes
      Render a noise as hidious and as loude,
      As a tumultuous sea in Tempest plow'd:
      When slaughter strowes the crimson plaine with Courses,
      Men combat men, inraged Horses, Horses:
      When Massacre, (all quarter quite denying)
      Revells amidst the flying, crying, dying.

      It is a Time when Stratagem surrounds, 480
      And the beleagured City close impounds:
      When mounted Ordnance with their streporous peale
      (Warrs Dialect) on both sides raile; and deale

136

Death at each dire discharge: When pinching need
Of food, hath forc'd the famish'd Mother feed
On her 'fore-starved Babe; and Hunger raves
So fiercely, Men eate men out of their Graves:
When Plague makes friend, the friend, brother, the brother;
The Harmlesse, armelesse, murder one another:
When in the Husbands and sad Parents sight,   As lately in
The Wife, and Virgins ravisht, in despight   Germany.
Of helpelesse succour; when without all ruth,
The Honourable Aged, lovely Youth
And Infant, in promiscuous heapes are throwne
(By indifferent havock) like a medow mowne.

     It is a time, when forrage, pillage, strage,
What witty cruelty, or barbarous rage
Can or invent or execute designe
To utter desolation: when in fine
Whole Troy is but one Bone-fire, that devours   500
House, Pallace, Temple, and kicks downe those Towers
That with the Clouds did late alliance boast;
Which in aspiring smoke give up the ghost.
Last, him (who Exit, in these Tragick Scenes),
Of sword, fire, famine, plagues find; thraldome gleanes.

     And such a time is War, and such the throwes
Our neighbour Nations travell now in; woes
Quite desperate of delivery: whilst calme Peace,
Prosperity, and Plenty, with increase
Of all concatinated Blessings smile   510
With cheerefull face on this sole-happy Isle.

     Let then our gratitudes and Pious cares
Strive to entaile them to Us, and our Heires:
Lest that too late, (having sterne Warre accited)
We wish that Peace; which (whilst we had) we slighted.

     One thing I cannot omit, concerning the Wardens and Committies of
this Worshipful Society of the Drapers; that howsoever in all my
writing I labour to avoyd what is Abstruse or obsolete: so withall I
study not to meddle with what is too frequent and common: yet in all
my expressions either of Poeticall fancie, or (more grave History),   520
their apprehensions went equally along with my reading: neither, had
I travel'd in the least deviating path, could I have escapt without a
just taxation: but I come now to the last Speech at night.

                         The last Speech.

The Sun is set, Day doth not now appeare

(As some few houres late) in our Hemisphere;
Hesperus the Captaine of the Watch, hath tane
Charge of the Starrs; and now about Charles-waine
Hath plac'd his Centinels to attend the Moone,
If possible to make of mid-night noone.   530

    May't please you to remember from old Nile,
The danger of th' Amphibian Crocadile;
How from old Janus, you this yeare have power
Over each Season, Moneth, each day and houre.
From Orpheus, that sweet musick of two parts,
The civill Harmony of tongues and hearts.
The Fleece of Aries Trumpets to eternity,
The Drapers Honour, due to that Fraternity.
We by the Sheep and Camels understand,
Your Lordships Travells both by Sea and Land: 540
Status Pacatus last doth intimate,
The happinesse of this your peacefull state.
Long may it last (of all Earths blessings best),
Whilst we this night commend you to your rest.

    Concerning these two excellent Artists, Master John, and Master
Mathias Christmas, brothers; the exquisite contrivers of these
Triumphall Models; I can onely say thus much: their workeman-ship
exceeds what I can expresse in words, and in my opinion their
performance of what they undertake, is equall at least, if not
transcendent over any's who in the like kind shall strive to   550
parralell them.

                        FINIS.

138

Londini Status Pacatus (Greg, Bibliography, no. 566; STC 13350),
Heywood's last mayoral pageant and the last until the Restoration, is
extant in six copies: Harvard University, Huntington, British
Library, Dyce Collection (Victoria and Albert), Bodleian, and the
Guildhall libraries. All have been collated; no press variants were
found. This text also appears in the 1874 Heywood edition, volume 5;
its significant alterations are recorded below in the Collation.

Collation

(title page) Maioralty] Majoralty Q, 1874

  3 Metropolis,] Metropolis; Q, 1874

 40 Lordships] Lordship 1874

 50 City] Gity 1874

 73 Maior] Major Q, 1874

 75 Maioralty] Majoralty Q, 1874

 79 Maior] Major Q, 1874

 88 Maior] 1874; Major Q

136 Watred] Waterd 1874

200 right] omitted, 1874

223 ope] O'pe Q, 1874

348 AEson] AEta Q, 1874

353 AEtes] AEta Q; Oetes 1874

400 excell] exceel 1874

421 last,] 1874; last. Q

468 astounded] assounded Q, 1874

471 Its] It's Q, 1874

518 Abstruse] 1874; Abtruse Q

529 to] to' Q, 1874

Commentary Notes

Sir Henry Garway's installation as mayor was celebrated by
Heywood's last mayoral pageant. This extravagant pageant cost the
guild £787. 3s. 4d. The request from the Drapers' guild parallels
the one that they had made in the previous year. The Christmas
brothers make all the arrangements, including lining up Heywood to
write the show. For their services they earn nearly £200. One
curious item in the records indicates a payment to Okes, the printer,
"for printing of Three hundred bookes for ye Companie over and above
ye number they were to have . . ." (Collections, p. 129). Whether
this means an unusual number of copies is difficult to determine
because of crucial blanks in the guild records. One interesting
historical footnote is the work of Richard Munday, paid for
"banners"; this son of the dramatist Anthony Munday first helped his
father back in the 1618 Lord Mayor's Show.

  2 Henry Garway] [or Garraway] sheriff 1627; Alderman
       Vintry and Broad Street; knighted 1640; died 1646 (see long
       entry in DNB).

 33 In Platoes Common-weale] see Plato's Republic.

 34 Acilius glabrio] M. Acilius Glabrio introduced the severe
       law that Heywood alludes to.

41-42 Embia al sabio . . . nada] "Send the wise man to the
       embassy and don't give/tell him anything." The Spanish is
       corrupt; the word "degat" in Heywood's quotation is
       unattested.

 43 Cato, Imperium gero . . . sociis.] "I hold power not for
       myself but for the state and its allies." Either Cato the
       Elder or the younger Cato is meant.

78-85 William Powltney . . . Henry Garway] see notes for the
       1638 pageant where all these former mayors are identified.

97-100 Crownes . . . blessed Virgin] all these items refer
       to the arms, motto, and patroness of the Drapers.

109 by Ovid, cald Septem-fluus] in Metamorphoses, Book I,
       line 422-3, "Sic ubi deseruit madidos septemfluus agros
       Nilus."

113 marle] a kind of soil, valuable as a fertilizer (OED).

115-116 Claudian thus expresseth: Et Arcanos Nili deprendite
       fontes] Claudian, Panegyricus de tertio Consulatu Honorii
       Agusti, 1. 207, "and surprise Nile's hidden spring."

140

116 Ecclesiasticall Writers] see the account in Genesis 2:11-14. The river "Gihon" is presumably the Nile. See also Jeremiah 2:18.

124f Crocadile is a Serpent] Heywood could have found such information in Pliny's Natural History, Book 8, chapter 26, pp. 208-10 (London, 1601). Pliny mentions that the Nile also has "River-horses."

142 Cremera] a small stream in Etruria which falls into the Tiber about six miles north of Rome.

144 Xautus, and Simois] Simois, small river in northwest Turkey, scene of legendary event in siege of Troy; Xanthus, a river of ancient Lydia.

148 Cephisus] name of several Greek rivers.

152 Pactolus nor Idaspes] Pactolus, small river in ancient Lydia (now Turkey). "Idaspes" is a medieval spelling of Hydaspes, which is the modern river Jeloum in India, a tributary of the Indus.

180f Janus] cf. Heywood's treatment of Janus in Gunaikeion, pp. 225-6, which notes that in Janus's right hand "hee had a golden key which opened the Temple of Peace, in his left, a staffe which hee strooke upon a stone, from whence a spring of water seemed to issue out. . . ."

242 off] meaning of, a fairly common spelling in Heywood. see l. 247 where of means off.

251 Orpheus with his Harpe] this description by Heywood corresponds closely with the traditional representation of Orpheus, especially in emblem books; see, for example, Whitney's A Choice of Emblemes (Leyden, 1586), in which the picture of Orpheus parallels in many respects Heywood's description. See the representation of Orpheus in Middleton's 1619 mayoral pageant.

299 Gitterne] a Cithern, a sort of guitar (OED).

328f Cammells there be two sorts] Heywood might readily have gotten such information from Edward Topsell's Historie of Four-Footed Beastes (London, 1607), pp. 92-99.

346-347 Jason, and Medea] the story of Jason and Medea is a familiar one in the pageants sponsored by the Drapers'; see, for example, Munday's 1615 show. Heywood had also dealt with the story in Canto VII of his Troia Britanica (1609).

348 Son of AEson] either Heywood or the printer got confused;
     both Jason and Medea cannot be the offspring of AEta. I
     have emended the text to show that AEson was the father of
     Jason, and AEtes (l. 353), the father of Medea.

392 were] an acceptable spelling for wear (OED).

427 strage] slaughter--see Heyood's use of this word in the
     1631 pageant, l. 112. (see also l. 496 below).

439 Pacem te poscimus omnes] we all ask you for peace.

446 by Plato, cald a more gentle and generous contention] in
     all likelihood a reference to the Republic.

490 (margin) As lately in Germany] reference to the
     destruction and devastation suffered by Germany in the
     Thirty Years' War.

514 accited] excited, aroused (OED).

A speech spoken before the right Honourable the Earle of Dover,

at his House at Hunsden, as a preparation to a Maske,

which consisted of nine Ladyes.

Presented the last New-yeares night.

London, 1637.

A speech spoken before the right Honourable the Earle of Dover,
at his House at Hunsden, as a preparation to a Maske,
which consisted of nine ladyes.
Presented the last New-yeares night.

The silver Swan soft gliding in the streame,
Cald to the Cocke then pearching on a beame,
And said to him; why, Chanticleere, when I
Move on the waves so low, thou sit'st so high?
The Cocke replide: O thou my best lov'd Sister
Well knowne in Poe, Meander, and Caister,   10
But best in Thamesis; Dost thou not know
The reason, why we in December crow?
More than before, or after? who againe
Thus answer'd: we of nothing can complaine
Being of all the birds that are, most white,
Loyall and chaste, and taking our delight
In rivers onely, bathing there our feete
To make our rare-heard musick sound more sweet.
Yet one thing to resolve, would make me proud,
To tell why at this time thou sing'st so lowd?   20
Who said: none of our ancestors but knew
That ever since Saint Peters Cock first crew,
We are injoyn'd to make lowd proclamation,
Of our most blessed Saviours Incarnation.
To which the Swan, (then in a Tone much higher)
Said, in this Caroll I will fill the quire:
Which being voyc't, did sound so sweet and shrill.
That where the Swan and Cock were heard, did fill
The ayre with such an eccho, thither came
Upon that summons, both the blind and lame,   30
Hungry and thirsty, poore, of all estates,
And none but fully sated at these gates.
Long may your bounty last, and we rejoyce,
To heare both City and the Country voyce
Your hospitality, to your loud fame,
Whilst Time indures, or Christmas beares a name.
And now great Lord and Lady both prepare,
To know what Sports in agitation are.

Truth presenting the Maskers.

Plaine Truth who onely hath the power   40
To steare the way to vertues bower,
By these cleare Tapers shining bright,
Doth celebrate this joviall night.

But by the Bird of <u>Mars</u> that crowes,
I now perceive the morning growes.
Her love to <u>Phoebus</u> to expresse,
And put his steeds in glorious dresse
Who shewes you what chaste virgins dwell,
Within the bosome of this Cell,
Appeare then O thou treble Trine   50
Of number, with the <u>Muses</u> nine.
(<u>Appolloes</u> sacred daughters) still
Frequent about <u>Pernassus</u> hill.
Of if you number them by Threes,
The first are the three <u>Charitees</u>,
Handmaides to <u>Venus</u>, <u>Graces</u> stil'd,
On whom their <u>Father Jove</u> still smil'd.
The second <u>Chorus</u> doth containe
Those beauties, by the <u>Trojan</u> swaine
On <u>Ida</u> judg'd: The third we call   60
The <u>Vertues</u> Theologicall,
<u>Faith</u>, <u>Hope</u>, and <u>Love</u>, haply meet here,
To crowne the parting of the yeare,
With Roses fresh of <u>Swan</u>-like hew,
Which from a royall <u>Stemme</u> first grew,
And the brave Yorkists long since bore,
These <u>vertues bower</u>, doe best decore,
Flowers redolent, which Heralds say,
<u>Janus</u> doth weare, as well as <u>May</u>.
Farre may they spread, be ever seene,   70
With milke white leaves, and branches greene,
Folded in amorous twines together,
Which <u>Winter</u> ne're may blast or wither.

Textual Notes

This fragment of a masque is found in Heywood's Pleasant
Dialogues and Drammas (STC 13358; London, 1637), pp. 245-247. I have
used the copy found in the Folger Shakespeare Library and have
collated it against the reprint in W. Bang's Materialien zur Kunde
des älteren Englischen Dramas (Louvain, 1903), vol. 3. This "masque
at Hunsdon" probably took place on 1 January 1637.

Commentary Notes

1 Earle of Dover] Henry Carey, son of John Carey, created
   Earl of Dover in March 1628; he died in April 1666. The
   whole volume of Pleasant Dialogues is dedicated to the Earl.
   Heywood's earlier Englands Elizabeth (1631) also contains a
   dedication to Carey.

10 Poe, Meander, and Caister] rivers first cited by Heywood
    in his 1632 Pageant (see the note there for lines 141f).

24 blessed Saviours Incarnation] This seems to echo the
    passage in Hamlet about the cock crowing. Marcellus
    observes: "Some say that ever 'gainst that season comes/
    Wherein our Saviour's birth is celebrated,/ This bird of
    dawning singeth all night long . . ." (I.i.158-160). The
    connection to Christmas is made explicit in l. 36 of
    Heywood's text.

39 Truth] cf. the appearance of Truth in the 1631 pageant.

56 Graces] see Heywood's discussion of the Graces in his
    Gunaikeion, pp. 107-108.

59-60 Trojan swaine On Ida judg'd] reference to the Judgment
       of Paris on Mount Ida at which time he chose Venus from
       among the three goddesses.

61 Vertues Theologicall] see Heywood's treatment of these
    Theological Graces in his 1633 pageant, l. 412.

66 brave Yorkists] reference to the War of the Roses in
    which the Yorkists chose the white rose as their emblem.

69 Janus] cf. the presentation of Janus in the 1639 pageant,
    ll. 180f.

For Product Safety Concerns and Information please contact our EU representative GPSR@taylorandfrancis.com Taylor & Francis Verlag GmbH, Kaufingerstraße 24, 80331 München, Germany

Printed and bound by CPI Group (UK) Ltd, Croydon, CR0 4YY

08/06/2025

01896979-0002